Tom, the Piper's Son

A Pantomime

Norman Robbins

Samuel French - London
New York - Toronto - Hollywood

FOR AMATEUR PRODUCTION ENQUIRIES

UNITED KINGDOM AND WORLD EXCLUDING NORTH AMERICA

plays@SamuelFrench-London.co.uk

020 7255 4302/01

Each title is subject to availability from Samuel French,

depending upon country of performance.

CHARACTERS

The Knave of Hearts
Fairy Harmony
Kitty Fisher, a village girl
Jack Horner, her beau
Tom Sprightly, the Piper's son
Dame Sprightly, his mother
Princess Marigold
The Lord Chamberlain
Georgie Porgie, the Dame's reluctant sweetheart
Buckett } two not so villainous villains
Spade
Herald
Old King Cole, the King of Hearts
Queen Mattiwilda, the Queen of Hearts
The Pieman
The Ship's Captain
Grendelgorm, the Guardian of the Sword
Chorus of **Villagers, Fayreground Vendors, Circus People, Courtiers, Soldiers, Sailors, Spirits of the Island, Chefs and Serving-wenches**
Babes Chorus

For Hannah Elizabeth

PROLOGUE

The Castle of the Knave of Hearts

ACT I

ACT II

MUSICAL NUMBERS

Please read the note on page viii.

ACT I
No. 1	**Villagers, Kitty, Jack**
No. 2	**Princess Marigold**
No. 3	**Tom**
No. 4	**Choristers**
No. 5	**Queen Mattiwilda**
No. 6	**Tom**
No. 7	**Children**
No. 8	**King Cole, Queen Mattiwilda, Choristers**
No. 9	**Tom**

ACT II
No. 10	**Sailors**
No. 11	**Princess Marigold, Children**
No. 11A (optional)	**Children**
No. 12	**Georgie, Dame Sprightly**
No. 13	**Spirits and Birds of the Island**
No. 14	**Tom**
No. 15	**Chefs, Serving-wenches**
No. 16	**Company**

Other Pantomimes by Norman Robbins
published by Samuel French Ltd

Aladdin
Ali Baba and the Forty Thieves
Cinderella
The Grand Old Duke of York
Hickory Dickory Dock
Humpty Dumpty
Rumplestiltzkin
Sing A Song Of Sixpence
The Sleeping Beauty
The Wonderful Story of Mother Goose

AUTHOR'S NOTE

The production of this pantomime is a pretty straightforward affair, and should present no great problems to experienced societies. For the benefit of others, however, perhaps the following notes will be of assistance.

All the scenes are full or lane-cloth scenes, one following the other. This gives a smooth flow to the action, for there should be little or no delay between scenes. Remember, the longer these changes are, the faster you lose your audiences' concentration.

The same reasoning applies to the dialogue. Keep it crisp and well paced. Not rushed, but most certainly not at a funeral pace.

The Tree of Truth

One of the oldest of our "traditional" pantomime gags, having almost as many variations as the tree has branches. Firstly the "fruit" must be large enough to recognize from the back of the theatre. Our apples were painted beachballs and trimming. If you can't manage apples, any other fruit or nut will work. Tennis balls painted orange (tangerines), plastic lemons, polystyrene coconuts, etc. The large branch that falls is quickly and easily made from wire (chicken or fencing) and covered with old newspaper and flour paste, painted to match the tree, and a few leaves and fruits.

The Sword on the Tree

There are several ways of making the sword appear on cue.

1. A pivoting trap set into the tree trunk. Painted to match the tree at both sides, the empty side faces the audience, the other side has spring clips fixed to it and the sword is pressed into them. On cue, and hidden by the flash, the trapdoor swivels, and the sword is "magically" revealed.

2. The sword is fixed to the tree on spring clips facing the audience. A painted cloth (both sides) matching the tree hangs over it, fastened at the *bottom*. Release pegs are at the top. On cue, the release pegs are withdrawn from behind the tree, the flap will fall under cover of the flash, and the sword appears as if by magic.

3. The sword is lowered from above on a fine nylon thread. If this is done, I suggest lowering it in the scabbard, so that Tom has only to unsheath it. The scabbard should be lavishly decorated.

The sword in all cases should be a broadsword. Others used are foils or épées.

Grendelgorm
In my original conception of this character, he is a Cyclopodic Giant.
However, an ordinary Giant will do quite nicely, but get one as fierce looking
as possible. He also needs a huge club. As a director of many years, though, I
realize it may not always be possible to hire a Giant's outfit for the period you
need, so a Dragon can be substituted without loss of tension. The offstage
roars (and onstage growls) should be done on an offstage microphone.

The Herald, or the Pieman, may double as the Captain or Grendelgorm.

The music used in the show
Over the past few years I've had many letters asking me what music I used in
my original productions, so, for guidance only, I have prepared a list of the
music for this pantomime which is obtainable from me, c/o Samuel French
Ltd. Remember though, it may not be suitable for your singers and some may
be out of print (local libraries can be of great help in obtaining vocal scores).
Also, please remember to contact the Performing Right Society before any
published music is used in your production. This is for your own protection.

Norman Robbins

PROLOGUE

The Castle of the Knave of Hearts

There is a dark lane cloth, eerily lit in blues, greens and reds. An ancient brazier stands down c glowing dimly. Behind the brazier, in magician's cloak and hat, is the Knave of Hearts, a grim, unlovable creature. With arms raised to just above shoulder height, and eyes gazing upwards, he speaks sonorously

Knave O dreadful demons that dwell within the enchanted flames of this eternal fire, draw near and reveal to me that which I, thy faithful servant, the Knave of Hearts, desire to know. Tell me: how can I break the magic spell that protects the land of Nursery-rhymes, and so take revenge on those who banished me to this dismal place? Speak. Speak, I beseech thee.

The light from the brazier grows brighter

See, the flame grows brighter. An immortal one is close. Soon I shall know the answer and Nursery-rhyme Land will be mine. All mine. (*He laughs harshly*) Twenty years have I waited for this moment. Twenty long years, trapped in this desolate wilderness, learning the secrets of the Black Art and plotting my revenge. (*He moves* R, *musing*) Well I remember that cursed day when they drove me out of the kingdom — and all for stealing a few paltry tartlets baked by that fool of a Queen, Mattiwilda. (*His voice rising*) How his royal incompetence King Cole had me beaten for my crime before he banished me, and how, with every passing year, I've grown to hate him more. (*Soberly*) And in all this time only one thing has prevented me from teaching him a lesson. The magic spell cast by the Fairy Queen to protect them from all danger. A spell that I — with all the demonic power I possess — have been unable to break. (*He snarls*) But now — NOW — I shall have the answer.

The brazier flares up very brightly

The Immortal One is here. (*He flings himself to his knees in obeisance, eyes downcast*)

Fairy Harmony enters R, *bathed in pure white light*

Fairy (*mischievously*) Such gallantry ... Though I suspect
        It isn't *me* that you expect.
Knave (*looking up, startled and annoyed*) The Fairy Harmony. (*He gets quickly to his feet, scowling*)
Fairy (*amused*) So once again to evil thoughts
        Your brain returns, my friend;

	I trust you've not forgotten
	I, that kingdom still defend?
	You'll never break the magic spell
	That guards their happy land.
Knave	Don't speak too soon, you simp'ring sprite.
	My time is close at hand.
Fairy	(*lightly*) But surely you must realize
	That whilst they do no wrong,
	The peaceful folk of Nursery-rhyme
	Are safe, secure and strong.
Knave	That's as may be. But should one soul
	Commit some wicked deed,
	The magic spell will *shatter*:
	For thus your Queen decreed.
Fairy	Quite so. But as each person there
	Is well aware of this,
	They never do a thing that's wrong
	And live in perfect bliss.

Knave (*aside*) Boring creatures. (*To her*) I'll prove you wrong, my smug young friend.

Fairy	You'll rue it if you try.
Knave	In Nursery-rhyme's clear ointment
	I intend to be the fly.
Fairy	(*sadly*) Then do your worst — but understand,
	You'll lose without a doubt.
	No help you'll get from yonder flame.
	(*She indicates the brazier*)

Knave Why not?

Fairy Because it's *out*.

She waves her wand as she speaks and the flame is extinguished at once

Fairy Harmony exits, laughing

Knave (*aghast*) My everlasting flame. (*He rushes over to it and attempts to blow life back without success*) Gone. Snuffed out like the flames of a common baker's oven. (*As a sudden thought strikes him*) But wait — wait. (*He ponders*) That *could* be the answer. The very idea I've been searching for. Yes. Yes. It *is*. (*Delightedly*) In seeking to outwit me, that stupid fairy has provided me with the perfect solution. Now I know exactly how to break that spell. By this time tomorrow, Nursery-rhyme Land will be *mine*. (*He laughs triumphantly*)

There is an instant Black-out

In the darkness, the Knave exits and the brazier is removed

The lane curtains open immediately on:

ACT I

Scene 1

The village of Tottering-on-the-Brink

A typical pantomime village setting of half-timbered cottages and shops. Dame Sprightly's cottage is UR and has a practical door

When the CURTAIN *rises, it is a bright, sunny morning, and the Villagers, led by Kitty Fisher and Jack Horner, are singing and dancing merrily*

SONG 1

As the song ends, Tom Sprightly, the Piper's son, enters UL and moves jauntily through the crowd, heading down C. He carries a large bundle of sticks to be used for firewood, and his pipes hang at his waist

Tom (*cheerily*) Hi, ev'rybody.

Villagers Hi, Tom.

Tom What's all the excitement, Jack Horner?

Jack (*stepping forward*) You mean you haven't heard the news? (*He looks at the others in amazement*)

Tom Not a word. As you can see, I've been out in the woods all morning gathering firewood to sell at the Fayre.

Jack (*with a grin*) Then have we got news for you. (*To Kitty*) Come on, Kitty. You tell him.

Kitty (*coming forward*) It's the Princess Marigold. She's coming here today to visit the Fayre. And as Jack's been chosen this year's Foreman of the Fayre, it'll be *his* job to escort her around.

Tom (*warmly*) Congratulations, Jack. (*To Kitty*) But if you'll take my advice, Kitty Fisher, you'll keep a sharp eye on Master Horner, here. I'm told the Princess is *rather* beautiful. (*He winks slyly*)

Jack (*laughing*) You don't have to worry about *me*. Kitty's the only one I care about. Besides, she's going to be my Queen of the Fayre, so I won't have much chance to make sheep's eyes at visiting princesses, will I? But what about you? We all know your reputation with the ladies, Tom Sprightly.

The Villagers agree with amusement

Tom (*ruefully*) I'm afraid there won't be much chance of *me* captivating the Princess. *I'll* be lucky to even get a glimpse of her. Mother's giving me so many jobs to do, it'll be a miracle if I ever get to the Fayreground in time to sell anything. (*He sighs*) Ah, well. I'd better be getting in before she comes looking for me.

Dame (*from inside the cottage*) Tom? Tom?

All react

Tom (*quickly*) Look-out. Here she comes now. Scatter. If she finds me here talking, she'll swear I've been wasting time instead of working.

There is an excited flurry as the Villagers, Kitty and Jack exit

Tom turns towards the cottage

Dame Sprightly comes charging out, still calling

Dame Tom? Where are you, you lazy good-for-nothing young——(*Seeing him*) Ahaaaaaa. There you are. (*She advances on him grimly*)

Tom (*brightly*) Oh, hello, Mum.

Dame Don't you "hello, Mum" me, you pipe-playing poltroon. Where do you think you've been hiding yourself all morning, eh? Don't tell me. I don't want to know. Five hours you've been gone. *Five hours*. And your lunch is ruined.

Tom (*dismayed*) Oh, no. And I'm starving. What was it?

Dame That special Australian dish your Uncle Fred sent me the recipe for.

Tom (*groaning*) Not *Boomerang Pie* again?

Dame (*on the defensive*) And what's wrong with my Boomerang Pie?

Tom Well . . . nothing. But it keeps coming back. (*He clutches his stomach*)

Dame (*starting to sniffle*) You want to think yourself lucky you get anything to eat at all. (*To the audience*) Oh, boys and girls, we're so poor, I have to take the bones out of my corsets to make soup with.

Tom (*contritely*) Don't cry, Mum. I didn't mean to criticize.

Dame (*sniffling*) I work my fingers to the bone, I do. And what do I get for it? Boney fingers. (*She dabs at her eyes*) It's no wonder I wake up every morning feeling homesick.

Tom (*surprised*) Homesick? But, Mum, you're *at* home.

Dame I know I am. And I'm sick of it. Here I am having to do everything on my own while you go gallivanting about the woods picking up sticks. (*She sobs*) Oooooh. It's all too much.

Tom I'm sorry, Mum. Really, I am. Was there *much* housework to do this morning?

Dame Housework? *Housework?* There's been nothing to do *but* housework. I've had to clean out the coal-house, hose out the hen-house, dust out the dog-house, wipe up the wash-house, and shine up the sh——ip's bell in the hallway.

Tom (*sighing*) Poor Mother. I've never known anyone work as hard as you do. If only poor Father were still alive.

Dame I know. But if he were, and he could see the mess we're in now, I swear he'd turn in his grave. (*She sighs*) Oh, I'll never forget the way he looked at me the last time I saw him.

Tom You mean – on the day he died?

Dame (*nodding*) Yes. I was cooking the dinner, and I asked him to go down

the garden and pick me a few sprouts. (*Fighting back the tears*) But before
he could move a muscle, he dropped down dead at me feet. (*She sobs*)

Tom (*aghast*) How awful for you. What on earth did you do?

Dame What *could* I do? I opened a tin of carrots, instead. (*Pulling herself
together*) Anyway, I don't know why we're standing out here in the street.
Let's go inside for a cup of tea and I'll show you all the old wedding
photos.

Tom (*surprised*) I didn't know you had any wedding photos, Mum. You've
never told me about them before.

Dame Haven't I? Oh, yes. We had them done by (*names local photographer*)
They were worth every penny we owed for them. You looked *beautiful* in
your little page-boy outfit.

*Tom looks startled. Dame Sprightly sweeps him quickly into the cottage,
chatting brightly. They exit*

Chamberlain (*off* UL, *shouting*) Your Highness . . . Your Highness. Wait.

Princess Marigold enters UL, *in a flurry of petticoats. She moves quickly
down* C *as the Chamberlain totters weakly into the square after her*

Your Highness . . . (*He gasps for breath*)

Princess (*turning to him*) No, no, no, no, no, no, *no*. I will *not* be escorted
everywhere I go, Lord Chamberlain, and that's final. If I can't go to the
Fayre alone, then I won't go at all.

Chamberlain (*pleading*) But, Your Highness . . . (*He staggers down to her*)

Princess (*kindly*) Oh, I'm not blaming *you*, Chamberlain. I know you're only
doing your job — (*firmly*) — but I refuse to be treated like a baby any
longer. I'm seventeen years old and quite capable of looking after myself.
Besides, what possible harm could come to me here in Nursery-rhyme
Land? It's the pleasantest place in the whole wide world.

Chamberlain I quite agree, Your Highness, and if it were up to me, why, I'd
let you wander around wherever you pleased. But — but — (*worried*)
whatever would Their Majesties say if I lost sight of you for even one
moment?

Princess They wouldn't say *anything* — if you didn't tell them. (*Pleading*) Oh,
Chamberlain. Can't you understand how much I hate being cooped up in
that stuffy old palace with no-one but the servants to talk to? (*Sadly*) I
never get to meet anyone *interesting*.

Chamberlain *Interesting*, Your Highness? Whatever do you mean?

Princess What I said. Interesting. (*Becoming dreamy*) Handsome, adorable;
intelligent, *passionate* young men. (*Coming out of her reverie*) The only
ones *I* seem to be introduced to are old and boring.

Chamberlain (*trying not to appear shocked*) Oh, come now, Your Highness.
What about the Prince of Diamonds? You can hardly call *him* old and boring.

Princess That's true. (*Grimacing*) But he's even worse. He's *young* and
boring. (*Turning away*) Oh, Chamberlain, whatever happened to all those
dashing young knights in shining white armour? Surely there must be one
of them left *somewhere*? (*She sings*)

SONG 2

Chamberlain (*kindly*) Never mind, Your Highness. I'm sure that one day the *right* young man will come along to claim you as his bride. But now you really *must* be making your way to the royal pavilion in the Fayreground. You'll have to change your gown before Their Majesties arrive.

Princess (*nodding sadly*) All right. (*She glances off* UL) Oh, here they come now.

Chamberlain (*startled*) What? (*He turns quickly to look off* UL)

As soon as his back is turned, the Princess gathers up her skirts and hurries off DR

(*Puzzled*) I don't *see* them, Your Highness. Are you sure? (*Pause*) Your Highness? Your *Highness*? (*He turns and sees she is missing*) *Your Highness?* (*He looks about wildly*) Oh, no. No. (*Calling in a panic*) Your Highness – come back. Come back.

He scuttles off UR, *calling anxiously. As he exits, Georgie Porgie enters* DL

Georgie (*seeing the audience*) Hiya, kids. (*He moves* C) Are you all enjoying yourselves? Are you? (*Audience reaction*) Why? What are you doing? (*He laughs*) My name is Georgie Porgie. Have you heard of me? Have you? (*Audience reaction*) Georgie Porgie, pudding and pie, kissed the girls and made them cry. (*He grins*) It's not true, you know. Not a word of it. I mean, do I *look* like the kind of feller who'd kiss the girls and make 'em cry, then run away when all the boys came out to play? Of course I don't. (*He chuckles*) I'd kiss all the *boys* as well. (*He laughs*) No, I'm only joking. To tell you the truth, I'm mad about girls, I am. Round here, I'm known as the local Don Juan. (*He grimaces*) The trouble is, the girls Don Juan anything to do with me. (*He chuckles again*) Anyway, as I was saying my name is Georgie Porgie and I live right here in Tottering-on-the-Brink. (*He indicates the village*) Funny little place, isn't it? All old-fashioned and out of date. In fact, it's just like (*names a local district*). Ahaaa——that surprised you, didn't it? You didn't think I knew about (*repeats the name*). Oh, yes. I know *all* about *that* place. (*He glances around to make sure he is not being overheard*) Think they're something special, round that way, don't they? All very *exclusive*. No local anaesthetics for that lot when *they* go to the dentists. They have 'em all imported. (*He grins*) But people are funny, aren't they? Well, they are in *this* village.

Dame Sprightly comes out of her cottage, all smiles

There's old Dame Sprightly, for instance. Now *there's* a funny woman.

Dame Sprightly stops dead in her tracks

Do you know, that woman has discovered the secret of eternal youth? It's true. She lies about her age. (*He grins*)

Dame Sprightly glowers

She had a birthday party last week and everybody was trying to count the candles on the cake to see how old she *really* was. But it wasn't any use. The heat kept driving them back. (*He laughs*) And what a *face*.

Dame Sprightly moves grimly down behind him

She's had it lifted so many times, she's only got to raise her eyebrows to pull her socks up. (*He falls about*) Here, and shall I tell you something else? She's been trying to get me to propose to her for the past ten years, but I've always been too — (*glancing sideways and seeing her glaring at him*) — oo — oo — oo ... (*quickly*) too *poor* to ask her to marry me. But now — NOW — it's going to be a different story.

Dame (*pushing back her sleeves*) Yes. You're going to be too *dead* to ask me.

Georgie (*edging away from her*) Now, now. Just a minute, Aubergine. You're making a terrible mistake.

Dame I know. And I'm just getting ready to *rub it out*. (*Savagely*) Stand still while I hit you. (*She waves her fists*)

Georgie (*warding her off*) Aubergine — listen. I'm going to get myself a *job*. Honest, I am.

Dame (*scornfully*) Get yourself a job? That's a laugh. You're so lazy, if you had the seven-year itch, you'd be six years behind with your scratching. Look at you. You swallowed a teaspoon twenty-five years ago, and haven't stirred since.

Georgie (*squirming*) Oh, give over. I've only got to be given the chance. I could be a real steady worker, I could.

Dame Steady worker? If you were any *more* steady, you'd be *motionless*. (*Softening slightly*) Anyway, it's no use trying to find a job around here. Don't you read the papers? There's thousands of jobs in jeopardy.

Georgie Well, that's all right. I'll go to Jeopardy. I don't mind travelling. (*He gives her a big false smile*) All I want to do is earn enough money for the two of us to get married.

Dame (*suspiciously*) Hurr. It's no use trying to pull the wool over *my* thighs. I heard what you were saying to the audience.

Georgie (*pushing her, playfully*) Oh, you don't want to take any notice of *that*. I was only joking. If you *really* want to know what I think of you, I'll tell you. You — are one of those rare women who have everything a red-blooded he-man could wish for.

Dame (*flattered*) Ohhhh. (*She preens herself*)

Georgie (*aside*) Bulging muscles, hairy arms, legs like tree trunks———

Dame (*sharply*) What was that?

Georgie (*innocently*) Nothing. Nothing at all. Honest.

Dame (*after a suspicious look*) Well, then, seeing as how we've cleared up that little misunderstanding, why don't we get a teensy bit closer and catch up on some kissing and cuddling? (*She simpers at him*)

Georgie (*startled*) Eh? You mean right now? In front of all *this* lot? (*He indicates the audience*) Oh, no, Aubergine. I couldn't. I'd be too embarrassed. They'd all laugh at me.

Dame No they wouldn't. (*To the audience*) would you? (*Audience reaction*) You see? (*She puckers her lips to him*) Come on, farmer. Plant one on this.

Georgie (*panic-stricken*) Look ... I mean ... wouldn't you — er — er ...

(*Quickly thinking*) Wait. Before I *do* kiss you, wouldn't you like to see the little *present* I've got for you?

Dame Present? For me? (*Eagerly*) What is it?

Georgie (*off-handedly*) Oh, it's nothing *special*. Just a pair of real, genuine, original "Lucky Knickers".

Dame (*startled*) "*Lucky Knickers*"?

Georgie Yes. I bought them this morning from one of the gypsies in the Fayreground. Only fifty p. (*He gets a paper bag out from under his coat*) Oh, but there is just one thing . . .

Dame (*drily*) I thought there might be.

Georgie I'm a bit short of money this week, so you'll have to give me the fifty p back.

Dame (*shrugging*) Oh, well . . . (*To the audience*) Fifty p isn't bad for a pair of "Lucky Knickers", is it, girls? (*She gets out a coin and gives it to him*) There you are. (*She takes the bag from him*) Oooh, I've never had a pair of these before and I could do with a bit of luck. (*She opens the bag and takes out a great big pair of bloomers with a large hole in them*) Here, there's a dirty great hole in 'em. (*She displays it*) I've been done.

Georgie (*grinning*) See? I told you they were lucky.

He dashes off, chased by a furious Dame Sprightly. As they exit, the Knave of Hearts enters with a harsh laugh

The Lights dim

Knave Once more the soil of Nursery-rhyme Land rests beneath my feet, and soon – very soon – shall I, the Knave of Hearts, take my rightful place as its Lord and Master, whilst the King and Queen lie rotting in the palace dungeons. (*He laughs*) But first I must find help. It's no use looking around here, though. Everyone is too good to be true. What I *need* is a couple of dyed-in-the-wool *crooks*. (*He muses*) Now which town councillors do I know? (*He snorts*) Pah. Why waste time with amateurs? I'll use my magic powers to find experts. (*He raises his arms*) Abracadabra, abracadee, two black-hearted villains deliver to me.

There is a great flash. The Lights flicker and die

Buckett and Spade tumble on to the stage

The Lights come up again as before

Buckett (*groaning*) Oooooooh. (*He picks himself up, weakly*)

Spade (*dazed*) What happened? Where are we? (*He staggers to his feet*)

Knave (*triumphantly*) Ahaaaaaa.

Buckett and Spade spin round to face him

Welcome to the land of Nursery-rhyme. (*He gives a mocking bow*) Permit me to introduce myself. (*Grandly*) The Knave of Hearts. Sultan of Sorcery, Wazir of Wizardry, Laureate of Legerdemaine, and Master of Magic.

Buckett (*impressed*) Cor.

Spade (*eagerly*) Here, do you know any card tricks?

Knave (*furiously*) Aghhhhhhhhhh.

He waves his arms as if to cast a spell and the men cower back in fright

Fool. Dolt. Imbecile. With the aid of my magic powers, I summoned you from afar to do my bidding. Do you understand? To do my bidding.

Buckett (*wide-eyed*) You mean there's going to be an auction?

Knave (*angrily*) Silence. One more word and you'll regret it for the rest of your miserable lives. (*He glares*) Now then: *will* you help me, or *won't* you?

Spade (*nervously*) Well—er ... What will we get if we do?

Knave (*smirking*) Gold, jewels, riches beyond belief.

Buckett And if we don't?

Knave (*drawing his index finger sharply across his throat*) Kkkkkkkkkkk.

Bucket and Spade glance quickly at each other

Buckett ⎫
Spade ⎰ (*together; repeating his action*) Kkkkkkkkkkk?

Knave (*nodding grimly*) Kkkkkkkkkkk. (*He repeats the action*)

Spade (*gulping*) W—w—what do we have to do?

Knave (*beaming*) First of all, I need to know your names. Who are you?

Buckett B-Benjamin Buckett, Your Magneticals.

Knave And? (*He glances at Spade*)

Spade Septimus S. Spade.

Knave (*curious*) What does the S stand for?

Spade Nothing. Me dad dropped a piece of spaghetti on my birth certificate.

Knave (*snorting*) Bah. Now tell me: are you both *genuine* villains? Nasty, evil, mean and vicious?

Buckett *What?* I'll say we are. Why, we've even been known to send "get well" cards to hypochondriacs.

Knave (*beaming*) Have you, indeed? Then it seems you're the perfect pair to help me with my plan. But remember. One word of this to anyone, and: (*drawing his finger sharply across his throat*) kkkkkkkkkkk.

Buckett and Spade react

Draw close whilst I whisper.

The three go into a huddle for a few moments then straighten

Have I made myself clear?

Buckett Leave it to us, Guv. Before this afternoon's out, *you'll* be the new King of Nursery-rhyme Land, and Old King Cole and his missis will be out on their ears.

Knave (*smirking*) Very well ... (*With sudden menace*) But should anything go wrong ...

Buckett ⎫ (*together*) ⎧ We know. (*Drawing their fingers sharply across their*
Spade   ⎰   ⎩ *throats*) Kkkkkkkkkkk.

Knave Till we meet again.

The Knave gives them a mocking bow and exits with a swirl of his cape

Spade (*pushing Buckett in annoyance*) Now look what you've done. What made you tell him we were a couple of villains? I thought we were trying to

go straight? When we last came out of prison, we promised the Chief
Warden we'd find honest jobs.
Buckett I know we did. I know. But who's going to be daft enough to employ
us? We've been out of work so long, we get invitations to the dole office
Christmas parties. Look, this is our chance to break into the big time. One
easy little job, and we could end up as the new King's official thieves.
Spade (*awed*) You mean we'd be running the Inland Revenue?
Buckett (*wincing*) Oooh. If ever the police put a price on your head, *take it*.
Come here. (*He pulls Spade closer*) Now according to our new boss, all we
have to do is to help him break this magic spell in the way he told us, and
we'll be rich for the rest of our lives. Right?
Spade Right. (*Uneasily*) But it's not being decent, though, is it? I mean,
breaking their magic spell. They haven't done anything wrong to us. (*To
the audience*) Here, kids, do *you* think we should help the Knave of Hearts?

Audience reaction

(*To Buckett*) You see?
Buckett (*to the audience*) You lot keep your mouths shut, or I'll put poison
in your ice-creams at the interval. (*To Spade*) Ahhhh, you don't want to
take any notice of *that* lot. I bet half of them haven't even paid to come in.
Now you listen to *me*.

Fairy Harmony enters DR

Fairy No.

Both turn to her, startled

> Heed him not. Whatever plot the Knave of Hearts doth hatch,
> His wicked deed shall *not* succeed. In *me* he'll meet his match.

Spade Here, who are you?
Fairy   Protectress of this happy place, as very soon you'll see.
> Pray let me introduce myself. The Fairy Harmony.
> (*She gives a slight curtsy*)

Buckett (*amused*) Fairy Harmony? Here, I know your sister. Fairy Liquid.
(*He falls about at his own wit*)
Fairy   (*ignoring him*) The Knave of Hearts, despite his hopes, once more
> shall come to grief:
> And those who choose to follow him, will find employment brief.
> Forget his boasting promises of "Never-empty purse".
> No rich reward you'll get from him, but banishment—or worse.
> So come. Accept my caution. Your commonsense display.
> Just tell me you'll renounce his plan, then gentlemen, good-day.

Buckett *Renounce it?* You've got to be kidding, missis. We're not going to
back out just because you come prancing around waggling your wand. Go
on. Clear off. And mind your own business.
Fairy (*firmly*) So be it. As you both elect my guidance to ignore,
> Misfortune shall attend your days; from this hour, evermore.
> Go. Do your worst. But think on this: I gave you warning fair.
> Adieu until we meet again. Though when we do—*beware*.

Fairy Harmony exits

Spade (*dismayed*) Here. No. Missis Fairy. Wait. (*To Buckett*) Oh, lor.
You've really gone and done it now, haven't you? That's all we need. A
fairy with a grudge against us.
Buckett Bah. You don't want to worry about her. If she were as tough as she
says she is, she wouldn't be trying to frighten us off, would she?
Spade (*nervously*) Wouldn't she?
Buckett Course she wouldn't. One wave of that wand and she'd have *made*
us do what she wanted. No. If you ask *me*, the Knave of Hearts chap has
got far stronger powers than her. And when we tell him what she's been up
to, he'll soon put her in her place. Now come on. Let's go find something to
eat before we set off for the Fayreground.

*Taking Spade's arm, Buckett tugs him off L. As they exit, Princess Marigold
enters, looking about her in bewilderment*

Princess (*dismayed*) The village square again. I must have gone round in a
circle. Oh, which is the right way to the Fayreground? If only there were
someone to ask.

Tom enters from the cottage carrying small bundles of firewood

(*Turning and seeing Tom*) Oh ... Excuse me.
Tom (*recognizing her*) Princess. (*He quickly drops to one knee and bows his
head*)
Princess Oh, please don't bother about all that. I'm sick and tired of looking
at the top of people's heads. I'd much rather look at their *faces.*
Tom .Well, in *that* case ... (*He springs to his feet, leaving his sticks on the
ground, and gazes at her*)
Princess I—er—I wonder if you can help me?
Tom (*gallantly*) Your wish is my command, Princess.
Princess (*slightly embarrassed*) Well, I—er—I'm afraid I've done something
rather silly, and managed to lose myself. I was with the Lord Chamberlain,
you see and——(*She breaks off*) Why are you staring at me?
Tom (*realizing*) Oh. I'm terribly sorry, Your Highness. Really, I am. It's just
that you're even *more* beautiful than I'd heard.
Princess (*lightly*) Why, thank you. (*Curiously*) What's your name?
Tom Tom, Your Highness. Tom Sprightly. The Piper's son.
Princess (*eagerly*) You mean there's a real piper living here in the village?
Tom I'm afraid not. Father passed away a long time ago. When I was only a
child.
Princess (*downcast*) Oh. (*Brightening*) But surely *you* can play the pipes? I see
you're carrying them in your belt. (*She indicates the pipes*)
Tom Well ... I *did* learn to play when I was young; but I only know the one
tune: "Over the hills and far away".
Princess (*delighted*) But that's my very favourite song. (*Eagerly*) Oh, Tom.
Do play it for me. Please.
Tom (*surprised*) You mean—here? Right now?
Princess Why not? We've got the whole village square to ourselves. Come
on. You play and I'll dance. (*She picks up her skirts and dances lightly*)

Tom (*uncomfortably*) Well, I really *would* like to play for you, Your Highness, but I have to be heading for the Fayreground. If I don't sell this firewood before nightfall, we'll have nothing to eat tomorrow.

Princess (*puzzled*) I don't understand.

Tom (*a little shamefaced*) Since Father died, this is how Mother and I live. If we don't sell our firewood, we starve.

Princess (*shocked*) But that's terrible. (*Brightening*) Look. Show me the way to the Fayreground and I'll ask my parents to give both you *and* your mother jobs at the palace. We're always needing help in the kitchens, so perhaps your mother would help in there, whilst you could be my very own court musician. Oh, Tom, you've no idea how boring it is having to listen to those three fiddlers scraping away all day. The pipes will be so much more fun.

Tom (*unable to believe his ears*) Do you really mean that, Princess?

Princess (*laughing*) Of course I do. (*Soberly*) On one condition.

Tom What is it?

Princess That you stop calling me "Princess" and "Your Highness', and call me by my real name, Marigold.

Tom (*unsure*) But would that be proper, Your Highness?

Princess I don't know. Though it *would* be very nice.

Tom Then I'll do it — Marigold.

Princess (*taking his hands eagerly*) Oh, Tom. You're the most interesting person I've met in my entire life, and I just know we're going to be wonderful friends, don't you?

Tom I sincerely hope so. But whatever happens, I know I'm going to remember this day for the rest of my life. (*He sings*)

SONG 3

After the song, Tom and the Princess move off towards the Fayreground

The Lights fade to Black-out and the lane cloth is brought in with as much speed as possible

SCENE 2

On the way to the Fayre

The Lights come up to full immediately on the lane cloth depicting a street or country setting

Dame Sprightly enters in a state of great excitement. She carries an open letter in one hand and clutches a shopping bag in the other, sticking out of the top of which is a pheasant's tail or chicken head and neck

Dame (*breathlessly*) Oh, boys and girls, such excitement. I've just had a letter from my sister (*names any film or TV beauty*). Oh, she's having a terrible time with that husband of hers. you know. (*Confidentially*) Between you and me, he's been doing some *very funny things* lately. (*She nods darkly*)

Right this very minute — as I'm standing here talking to you — she's got fifteen psychiatrists working on him to find out what makes him tick. *And* why he chimes every quarter of an hour. Still, I've had this letter and I'll tell you what it says. (*Reading*) "Dear Aubergine, I know you haven't much money for food, so I'm sending you this beautiful pheasant for Sunday dinner. (*She displays the bag*) Hope you like it. (*Excitedly*) Ooooh, isn't it kind of her? Sending me a present of a pheasant. Honestly, I'm so excited about it, I haven't even had time to see if it's going to be big enough for two. I'd better just check. (*She opens the bag and sticks her nose inside*) Ooooooooooooh. (*She staggers back gasping for air*) What a terrible smell. It must have died of the Black Death. Ohhhhh, I shall have to get rid of it. We can't eat *that*. (*She holds the bag away from her*) Good heavens. Ohhhhhhhh.

The Chamberlain enters, looking around worriedly

Chamberlain Oh, dear, oh, dear. I can't find the Princess anywhere. Whatever am I going to do?
Dame (*spotting him*) Oh. It's Neville — the Chamberlain. (*To the audience*) Shhhh. I'll give it to him. (*To the Chamberlain*) Yoo-hoo.
Chamberlain (*noticing her*) Oh, hello, Dame Sprightly. (*He looks behind him*)
Dame (*curious*) Is something wrong?
Chamberlain (*startled*) Wrong? Wrong? No, of course not. Why should there be?
Dame Well, you look as white as a sheet. Feel your face and see.
Chamberlain (*gingerly touching his cheek*) Oh, dear. You're absolutely right.
Dame (*kindly*) Still, there's nothing to worry about. All you need is a nice bit of pheasant inside you. It'll do you the world of good. Here. Because you're such a lovely man, I'm going to give you one. (*She hands over the bag*) A present of a pheasant. Happy eating.

Dame Sprightly scuttles off quickly

Chamberlain (*flattered*) Well. Isn't that kind of Dame Sprightly? Fancy giving me a pheasant. Now if only I can find the Princess, perhaps I can persuade her to join me for dinner tonight. I'm sure it'll be big enough for two. I'll just have a peep. (*He opens the bag, and sticks his nose in*) Ooooooooooh. (*He reels back in horror*) What a revolting smell. (*He holds the bag away from him*) What a very unpleasant pheasant. Ohhhhhhhh, I shall have to get rid of it.

Buckett and Spade enter

Spade (*groaning*) Oh, I'm absolutely starving.
Buckett Me too. We've got to get something to eat or we won't even *live* to do the job. (*He sees the Chamberlain*) Look. Let's see if we can beg something from *him*.

They hurry over to the Chamberlain

'Scuse us, Guv.
Chamberlain (*turning*) Yes?

Spade (*pleading*) Spare a few pence for a couple of starving tramps.
Buckett We haven't eaten for over a week.
Chamberlain (*taken aback*) Good heavens. Beggars. (*He turns up his nose*) You aught to be ashamed of yourselves. Begging in *this* neighbourhood.
Spade Oh, there's no need to *apologize* for it. We've seen *much* worse.

The Chamberlain is about to reply in indignation when he remembers the pheasant

Chamberlain (*smiling thinly*) Tell me, do you like pheasant?

Buckett and Spade look at each other in delight

Buckett ⎫
Spade ⎭ (*together*) We certainly do.

Chamberlain (*beaming*) Very well, then. Take *this* one.

The Chamberlain hands them the bag and hurries off, chuckling

Buckett (*enraptured*) A pheasant. A pheasant. He gave us a pheasant. (*He pauses and gives a loud sniff, looking around as he does so*)
Spade (*curious*) What's wrong? (*He too sniffs the air*) Cor, what a terrible smell. I wonder where it's coming from? (*He peers around*)

Buckett opens the bag, sticks his nose inside, then staggers back

Buckett (*staggering back*) Gaaaaaaaaaah. (*He pushes the bag at Spade*)
Spade (*startled*) Eh? (*He sticks his nose inside it, then reels back*) Ughhhhhhhh. (*He pushes the bag back at Buckett*) Cor, blimey. Take it away. Ohhhhhhhhhhh.
Buckett (*holding the bag away from him*) We can't eat that. It's rotten. No wonder he was so eager to get rid of it. Phewwwww. What are we going to do with it?

Georgie enters

Georgie (*to the audience*) Hiya, kids.
Spade (*nudging Buckett*) Here, this one looks a bit simple. Let's give it to him.
Buckett Good idea. (*He hides the bag behind his back and moves to Georgie*) I say . . .
Georgie (*turning to him*) Yes?
Buckett You—er—you wouldn't be feeling hungry, would you?
Georgie Hungry? I'm absolutely starving. As a matter of fact I was just on me way to (*names a local café*) for a bowl of enthusiastic stew.
Spade (*blankly*) Enthusiastic stew?
Georgie Yes. They put everything they've got into it. (*He chuckles*)
Buckett (*dryly*) Ho, ho. Very droll. (*Brightly*) Forget about stew. *We've* got something far better than stew for you. A nice fat pheasant.
Georgie (*excitedly to the audience*) Oooh, did you hear that, kids? They've got a nice fat pheasant for me. (*To Buckett*) Oooooh, I love pheasant.

Buckett How fortuitous. Well, here you are then. (*He hands over the bag*) One pheasant. A gift from Buckett and Spade.
Spade Happy eating.

Buckett and Spade snigger and exit quickly

Georgie (*to the audience*) Hey, fancy that. Two perfect strangers giving me a present of a pheasant. Wasn't that kind of them? (*Audience reaction*) Eh? What do you mean, "no"? Of course it was. It's very expensive, pheasant is, and it's not every day that somebody comes up to you and . . . (*He sniffs suspiciously. He looks down at the floor around him, then checks the soles of his shoes. Seeing nothing, he begins to speak to the audience again*) I mean, it's so long since I . . . (*He sniffs again and looks down into the orchestra*) There's a funny smell up here tonight. It's not something you're wearing, is it? No? (*He looks at the front row*) Is it you, missis? Are you sure? Eh? It's what? In the bag? (*He opens the bag, sniffs inside it and reels back*) Oooooooooh. Good heavens. Cor. What a terrible smell. Oooooooooh. I shall have to get rid of it. Oh, dear. Ohhhhhhhhhhhh.

Holding the bag at arm's length, Georgie exits quickly. As he does so, Dame Sprightly comes hurrying on at the opposite side. She is panic-stricken and is clutching the letter

Dame (*gasping*) Oh, boys and girls. I'm in terrible trouble. I've just read the last bit of this letter from my sister, and she says: (*reading the letter*) "P.S. Inside the pheasant is a *five-pound note*." Ohhhh, I've got to get it back. Now who did I give it to? (*She thinks furiously*)

The Chamberlain enters from the opposite side

Oh, yes. (*She hurries over to him*) The very man I've been looking for. You remember a few minutes ago, I gave you a pheasant?
Chamberlain (*embarrassed*) Oh – er – yes. Yes.
Dame Well I've got to get it back. What have you done with it? (*She begins to search him*)
Chamberlain (*fighting her off*) Please, Dame Sprightly, control yourself. As a matter of fact, I – er – I passed it on to a couple of starving beggars.
Dame (*groaning*) Oh, no.
Chamberlain (*curious*) What's the matter?
Dame Inside the pheasant was a five-pound note.
Chamberlain (*dismayed*) What? (*He groans*) Oh, no. (*He looks around anxiously*) Which way did they go?

Buckett and Spade enter opposite

Ah, rejoicings. (*He hurries to them*) Gentlemen. About the pheasant I gave you recently. You haven't eaten it, have you?
Buckett Are you kidding? You wouldn't catch *us* eating a thing like that.
Spade I'll say. It was absolutely rotten.
Chamberlain (*in mock surprise*) Was it? Well, in that case, perhaps you wouldn't mind letting me have it back? (*Off-handedly*) It – er – it was an old family heirloom, you see.

Buckett I don't care what it was. You're too late. We've given it to somebody else.

Chamberlain ⎫
Dame ⎭ *(together)* Oh, no.

Spade What's the matter?

Chamberlain ⎫
Dame ⎭ *(together)* Inside the pheasant was a five-pound note.

Buckett ⎫
Spade ⎭ *(together)* What? *(They groan)* Quick. We've got to get it back.

Georgie enters, still holding the bag at arm's length

Buckett *(snatching it off him)* I've got the pheasant. *(He holds up the bag)*
Spade *(snatching it)* I've got the pheasant. *(He holds up the bag)*
Chamberlain *(snatching it)* I've got the pheasant. *(He holds up the bag)*
Dame *(snatching it)* I've got the pheasant. *(She clutches it to her fiercely)*
Georgie Yes. But I've got the five-pound note. *(He waves it aloft)*

All shriek with rage and chase him off

Black-out

SCENE 3

The Fayreground

The Lights come up on a backdrop of gaily painted tents, sideshows, caravans and stalls, set against a background of hills and trees. A troup of Circus Performers are entertaining the crowd, whilst Vendors move about carrying display trays of toys, balloons, doughnuts, candy-floss, etc. As this is going on, a bright bouncy song is sung

SONG 4

At the end of the song a fanfare is heard

A Herald enters UC

Herald *(grandly)* Their Most Glorious Majesties, Old King Cole and Queen Mattiwilda, King and Queen of Hearts.

The crowd cheer loudly

King Cole and Queen Mattiwilda enter UC. *They have long since passed their prime, but the Queen's visage remains a triumph of Art over Nature*

As the hubbub continues around them, the royal couple move downstage, smiling and waving

Queen *(loudly, but with extreme refinement)* A-hem . . .

The noise stops at once

My husband and I——

King (*tapping her shoulder gently*) Mattiwilda, dear, I'll do the commercials. (*He beams at her*)

Queen (*blinking*) Oh. (*She shrugs*) Very well, beloved. Just as you please.

King (*beaming at the crowd*) Her husband and I . . . (*He winces*) My husband and I . . . I mean . . . we have great pleasure in once again being able to visit our very favourite part of the kingdom: this tiny village of er er er . . . (*He flounders*)

Queen (*hissing at him*) Tottering, dear. Tottering-on-the-Brink.

King (*recovering*) Oh, yes. Tottering-on-the-Brink. (*He beams at everyone*) My, my. We *have* had some fun here in the past, haven't we, Matti?

Queen We certainly have. Why, I still remember our coming here eighteen years ago. The very last time we visited the Fayre. You entered the "Knobbliest Knees" competition AND won first prize—that *enormous* box of Garden of Eden cigars.

King (*remembering*) Oh, yes. And now I know *why* they called them Garden of Eden cigars. Once I'd 'ad 'em, I 'eaved. (*He holds his stomach*)

The crowd look amused

Still, that's all in the past. Let's get on with the present. (*He looks around*) Where's the Foreman of the Fayre?

Jack enters in his "official costume", leading Kitty, who wears a "Queen of the Fayre" gown

Jack Here I am, Your Majesties. Jack Horner, at your service, and Miss Kitty Fisher, my chosen "Queen of the Fayre".

Both defer to the royal pair

King (*beaming*) Tell me, Master Horner, have all the preparations been prepared?

Jack (*brightly*) Indeed they have, Your Majesty. In fact, the royal pavilion is surrounded by people waiting to welcome you, so if you'd care to step this way . . . (*He indicates*)

King Oh—er—well . . . There's something I'd like to discuss with the Queen first. In private. Why don't you take everyone else along and come back for us in a few minutes?

Jack As Your Majesty wishes.

Jack bows to the royal pair, as do the rest of the crowd, then all exit, leaving the King and Queen alone

Queen Oh, Aloysius, what a pretty young girl that Mistress Fisher is. I wonder if I should offer her a job at the palace? I've got half a mind, you know.

King It's good of you to admit it, dear, but the answer's *no*. The palace is full of pretty girls. (*Sternly*) It's got to stop, Matti. Right this very minute. Understand?

Queen (*blankly*) What has, dear?

King All this reckless spending. We simply can't *afford* any more servants. The royal treasury is almost as bare as Mother Hubbard's cupboard, and if we carrry on spending as we have been doing, I *may* have to pawn the crown jewels.

Queen (*dismayed*) Oh, no.

King Far be it from me to criticize, dear, but you've run up so many bills in the last few months, I'll be lucky if I can scrape enough cash together to settle them.

Queen Well, it *is* partly your *own* fault, darling. After all, when you first proposed to me, you said I'd be able to share your wealth for the rest of my life.

King I know. But I thought you'd be sharing it with *me*, not the hairdresser, the beauty parlours and the dress shops.

Queen (*protesting gently*) But, Aloysius, I have to keep up appearances. As Queen of Nursery-rhyme Land, the people expect me to set an example. For instance, if flowery hats are in fashion, then *my* hat must have more flowers on it than anyone else's.

King (*wincing*) You don't have to remind me. Look at the one you wore for the Easter parade. There were so many flowers on *that* one, when we left the parade to return home, we were followed by sixteen funeral cars. (*He sighs*) Oh, if only there were some way we could raise a spot of cash.

Queen (*brightly*) I know. Why don't I mix up a batch of my special jam tarts and sell them to the highest bidder?

King (*firmly*) No. I absolutely forbid it. You know perfectly well what happened the *last* time you baked jam tarts. That nasty little Knave came along and stole them clean away.

Queen But that was twenty years ago. Oh, Aloysius, just think of the excitement it would cause. The first jam tarts I'd made since that terrible day. People would pay a fortune for them.

King And what would happen if someone else gave in to temptation and stole them? We'd lose our fairy protection and perhaps the kingdom too. No. Something's bound to turn up, so don't you worry your pretty little head about it. But just for the moment no more spending, Hmm?

Queen (*nodding*) Very well, dear. (*Suddenly*) Oh, but what about the Ball tonight? I haven't a single thing to wear.

King Matti. Your wardrobes are so packed out with clothing, you've got moths inside them who've never learned to fly.

She looks at him sorrowfully

Oh, very well. You can buy something for tonight.

Queen (*delightedly*) Oh, thank you, darling. As soon as the Fayre ends, I'll catch the first sedan chair to London.

King (*startled*) London? *London?* Why on earth do you have to go to London for a dress? You can buy a thousand different dresses right here in (*names the town the performance is taking place in*).

Queen (*eyes widening*) I can? (*She flings her arms around him*) Oh, you're so generous, Aloysius. (*She dances away from him*) Thank you, my dear. Thank you very much.

As the bewildered King flounders, Queen Mattiwilda burst into:

SONG 5

*As she sings, Jack, Kitty and the Choristers enter and join in the song. At the
end of it, all exit happily, the Queen escorting the dazed King*

The Lights dim

The Knave enters DL

Knave (*sneering*) So, their Royal Highnesses are short of money, are they?
Things look better and better with every passing minute. Now where are
those two idiots I hired to help me?

Buckett and Spade enter

Spade Here we are, boss. Ready and willing.
Knave (*snarling*) You're late.
Buckett Sorry about that. But we were just coming through Sherwood
Forest when we were taken by surprise by Robin Hood.
Knave Robin Hood?
Spade Yes. He wanted us to join his band, but we hadn't got enough money
to buy the instruments.

Buckett and Spade curl up with laughter

Knave (*sourly*) Bah. Is everything ready?
Buckett Oh, yes, Guv'nor.
Spade Just as you told us.
Knave Good. Then in five minutes time, we *strike*. (*He rubs his hands*)
Buckett Blimey. He took the words right out of (*Union leader's*) mouth.
Knave Away with you and prepare yourselves.

Buckett and Spade exit quickly

How fitting it is that here, in the self-same Fayreground that saw me
banished, I now return to take my revenge.

> The wheel of Fortune spins again. My destiny awaits.
> No longer shall my future lie in hands of unknown Fates.
> From this day on, I'll rule supreme: *whatever* may befall.
> The Knave of Hearts is home again, and *master over all.*

Giving a harsh, triumphant laugh, he exits

The Lights come up to full again

Tom and the Princess enter

Princess (*as she enters*) Now I *know* you're teasing me. Up to his middle,
indeed. (*She laughs lightly*)
Tom (*leading her down stage*) But it's true. Honestly, it is. (*He laughs*) And he
never went there again.

They laugh together

Princess Poor Doctor Foster. How I *wish* I'd been there to see it. (*She wipes* *away a laughter tear*) Oh, Tom, you really do know the funniest stories. It's going to be marvellous having you at the palace with us. I can't *wait* to introduce you to Mother and Father. (*She looks around*) Which way is it to the royal pavilion?

Tom (*indicating*) Through there, but hadn't you first better find the Lord Chamberlain and let him know you've arrived here safely? He's bound to be worrying.

Princess (*wryly*) I suppose you're right. He won't have had a minute's peace since I ran away from him, though you'd think he'd be quite used to it by now.

Tom (*laughing*) You mean you run away often?

Princess Whenever I get the chance. (*Glumly*) There's absolutely *nothing* to do in the palace, except sit around in a pretty dress, waiting for some boring old prince to arrive and ask for my hand in marriage.

Tom And—does *that* happen often?

Princess At least twice a week. And what's even *more* boring they all claim to love me twice as much as the one before. (*She sighs*) I sometimes feel I must be the most loved person in the entire world.

Tom (*amused*) Well, that's nothing to look so gloomy about. It must be rather flattering to be told that somebody loves you.

Princess Only if it's true. It doesn't mean a thing when you know that even as they're saying it, they're busy counting the diamonds in your necklace. (*She turns away downcast*) If I wasn't a princess, I just know that no-one would ever look twice at me.

Tom Oh, but you're wrong, Marigold. Absolutely wrong. *I'd* look twice at you *any* time.

She turns back to face him, pleased

You see, I too fell in love with you. The moment I set eyes on you. And even though I know it's impossible for you to feel the same way about me, I'll never love anyone else for the rest of my life.

Princess Why should it be impossible?

Tom Well, you're a princess, and I'm a pauper. How could you possibly love *me*? And besides, even if you did, we'd never be able to marry. Your parents would never agree to it.

Princess (*eagerly*) They would if you rescued me from a giant, or saved the kingdom from a terrible dragon.

Tom (*laughing*) I'm afraid there's not much hope of *that* happening. So long as the magic spell holds fast, we won't even be menaced by (*names unpopular personality in the public eye*), let alone a giant or dragon.

Princess (*annoyed*) Oh, I hate that stupid spell. (*Miserably*) Nothing's ever going to happen in Nursery-rhyme Land until it's broken. We'll all grow old without once having had a single, solitary adventure. Oh, Tom, I'd sooner marry you than a thousand stuffy old princes. Truly, I would.

Tom (*stunned*) You don't *mean* that? Not *really*?

Princess Yes, I do. And if I can't marry you, I swear I won't marry anyone. (*Dejectedly*) The only trouble is, unless you can somehow find fame and fortune, we'll never be able to be more than just good friends.

Tom (*boldly*) Don't worry about *that*, Marigold. Now I know that *you* love *me*, fame and fortune are going to come running. Before the year is out, I'm going to be richer than Aladdin.

Princess But how?

Tom I'm not sure, but with you behind me, there's going to be nothing I can't do. (*He sings*)

SONG 6

After the song, they exit towards the royal pavilion. As they do so, Dame enters DR *in a startling "frock"*

Dame (*to the audience*) Do you like the frock, girls? (*She parades it*) It's a Dorothy Perkins bargain. Mind you, I had a terrible time finding it. Some of the clothes they're selling these days. I've seen more cotton in the top of an asprin bottle. There was one dress—I must tell you about it—that was so *skimpy*, I couldn't tell if it had a low neckline or a high hem. Ohhhh, and the woman that bought it. What a snooty, stuck-up cat *she* was. Do you know, she looked at me as though I was as common as muck. But it didn't upset me. I just looked right back at her as though I wasn't.

George enters L, *wearing a "strong-man" outfit*

Georgie (*to the audience*) Hiya, kids. (*He strikes a pose*) Hello, Aubergine.

As the Dame looks on in amazement, he executes a series of comical muscle-man poses, accompanied by grunts, groans and wheezes of exertion

Dame (*after a moment*) I say, Tarzan.

He stops his work-out and looks at her innocently

I don't wish to appear *inquisitive*, but would you mind telling me exactly what it is you're supposed to be doing?

Georgie (*in a tough-guy tone*) Pumping iron, sister. Pumping iron.

Dame (*grimly*) I don't know about *pumping* iron, but you'll be getting a lump of it wrapped around your ear-hole in a minute. (*Fiercely*) What do you think you're playing at? Stood standing in the middle of a public fayreground wearing nothing but a set of goose-pimples and one of my living-room curtains.

Georgie (*nervously*) Oh—well—er—I—er—I was just airing my muscles.

Dame (*snorting*) Muscles? You call them things *muscles*? They look more like gnat bites on sticks of spaghetti. Go put your clothes on before somebody comes along and sees you. You'll have 'em thinking it's Halloween.

Georgie (*protesting*) But I *want* 'em to see me, Aubergine. I mean, I've got to look like this if I'm going to apply for the job.

Dame What job?

Georgie The one they're advertising outside the circus tent. "Strong man wanted."

Dame (*looking at him askance*) Strong man? You don't mean to tell me that you're hoping to get it, do you? With a physique like that?

Georgie (*puzzled*) What's wrong with me physique? (*He looks down at himself*)

Dame Well, far be it from me to crystallize, but if it wasn't for your Adam's apple, you wouldn't have a shape at all. I've seen better bodies on second-hand cars. Look at you. Anaemia on legs. If you cut yourself, you'd have to have a transfusion before you could bleed.

Georgie (*embarrassed*) Oh, give over.

Dame (*patiently*) Listen, pudding-head. If you want to be a *real* strong man, you've got to do exercises. The most *you've* done lately is to watch horror films and let your flesh creep. And another thing, you've got to eat special foods. Raw meat, protein, oysters ...

Georgie (*quickly*) Oh, I've been eating oysters. As a matter of fact, I had four dozen of 'em about half an hour ago. (*Uneasily*) Mind you, I'm starting to wish I hadn't. I feel ever so sick.

Dame (*startled*) Eh? (*Concerned*) Oh, dear. There was nothing wrong with them, was there? I mean, they *were* all fresh?

Georgie (*doubtfully*) I suppose so. I don't know. (*He holds his stomach*)

Dame What do you mean, you don't know? What did they look like when you opened them?

Georgie (*blinking*) Eh? Do you mean you've got to *open* them? Ooooooooh.

Dame (*tiredly; to the audience*) Honestly. If brains were gunpowder, he wouldn't have enough to blow his hat off. (*To Georgie*) Hoy, Mighty Mouse, why do you want a job in a circus, anyway?

Georgie Well, it's in me blood, isn't it? It's "show business" (*He sings*) "There's no business like show business, like no business I know"——

Dame (*cutting in*) I didn't know you were interested in show business.

Georgie Oh, yes. I once had an uncle who worked in the theatre. Marvo the Magnificent, Master of Disguise.

Dame Master of disguise? Was he any good?

Georgie Good? He was fantastic. Do you know, one day he made himself up to look like Abraham Lincoln. He *looked* like him, he *dressed* like him, he *walked* like him and he *talked* like him.

Dame (*impressed*) Oooh. I bet he fooled a few people, didn't he?

Georgie I'll say he did. On the way to the theatre, somebody shot him.

The Dame hits him about the head and shoulders and chases him off. As they exit, Villagers begin to enter, chatting brightly. Vendors also appear, crying their wares, and the Villagers cluster around to inspect or sample. Jack and Kitty enter hand in hand

Kitty (*happily*) Oh, Jack. We couldn't have had a better day for the fayre if we'd chosen it ourselves. It's absolutely perfect.

Jack Well, everything seems to be running smoothly, and the King and Queen appear happy enough. Come on. Let me buy you an ice-cream.

They start to move off

The Pieman appears UC. He is carrying a large display tray, piled high with pastry pigs, and is followed by a crowd of small Children

Pieman (*calling*) Pastry pigs. Pastry pigs. Filled with mincemeat and spices.
Kitty (*eagerly*) I'd rather have one of those, if you don't mind.
Jack Why not? (*Calling*) Mr Pieman. (*He signals to him*)

The Pieman moves down to them, followed by the Children

One of your pastry pigs, if you please.
Pieman (*beaming*) Long or short-tailed, sir? (*He holds up one of each*)
kitty (*laughing*) It doesn't really matter, so long as they're tasty.
Pieman Oh, they're tasty all right, miss. Finest pigs in the whole of Nursery-
rhyme Land, and only one penny each.
Kitty (*undecided*) Now which shall it be? (*To the children*) Come on,
children. Help me to decide. Long-tailed or short?

*The Children offer various choices, but one little girl remains downcast and
silent*

(*To her*) And what about *you*, little girl? Which one do *you* think I should
choose?
Girl Please, miss, I don't know. I've never ever tasted one.
Kitty (*surprised*) You haven't? Oh, we can't have that, can we? (*Brightly*)
I'll tell you what. You choose one for me, and we'll both share it.

The girl jumps for joy, but the other children burst into tears

(*Startled*) What's wrong?
2nd Child *We've* never tasted one, either.
Jack (*laughing*) All right, then. Dry your tears. (*To the Pieman*) Pastry pigs
for all of them, Mr Pieman. And I'll pay.

The Children cheer loudly and eagerly choose a pig. Jack pays

Kitty Now, children, what do you say?
Children Thank you, Master Horner.
3rd Child And if there's ever anything we can do for you ...
Jack (*laughing*) Well, as a matter of fact, I think there *might* be. How about
taking a leaf from Tommy Tucker's book, and repaying me with a song?

Everyone around agrees

4th Child All right. (*To the conductor or pianist*) Music, maestro, please.

SONG 7

*The Children sing. Kitty, Jack, the Pieman and others may join in if required.
At the end of the song, all applaud the Children*

Jack And now, in my official capacity as Foreman of the Fayre, I invite
everybody to join me for a cold drink in the refreshment tent.

There are loud cheers from all

*Kitty and Jack exit followed by the crowd. The Pieman slips off his tray and
places it UC before following them. As soon as he is gone, Buckett and Spade*

enter. Buckett is dressed as a Pieman, and Spade as a schoolboy in short trousers

Buckett (*crossing to the tray and picking it up*) The very thing we're looking for. Keep an eye out for a suitable victim.
Spade (*looking off*) There's somebody coming now.
Buckett Right. (*Calling*) Pastry pigs. Pastry pigs. Get your pastry pigs right here.

Tom enters and begins to cross

Spade (*stopping him*) Excuse me, mister. Spare a penny for a pastry pig.
Tom (*ruefully*) I'm sorry, little boy. I haven't got a penny in the world.
Spade (*shedding mock tears*) I wanna pastry pig. (*He bawls*)
Tom (*kindly*) Oh, there, there. Don't cry. (*He looks at Buckett alias the Pieman*) Look. You wait here and I'll see what I can do. (*He moves up to Buckett*) I—er—I don't suppose you'd be willing to give one of your pastry pigs to that little boy over there, would you? He looks so hungry, but he hasn't any money. Neither have I, for that matter.
Buckett (*beaming*) Money? Money? You don't need money for *my* pigs, young sir. Just for today, all *my* pigs are *free*.
Tom (*amazed*) *Free?* You mean he can help himself?
Buckett Just for today. Tomorrow they'll be a penny each again. (*He offers the tray*) Here. I've only three left. Take one for him and have one yourself.
Tom (*delightedly*) Why, thank you. (*He takes two*) They really *do* look delicious. (*He takes one to Spade*) Here, little boy. And don't forget to say thank you to the kind Pieman. (*He begins to exit*) Free pigs. I can hardly believe it. Wait till I tell Mother.

Tom hurries off

As soon as he is gone, Spade hurries up to Buckett and replaces the pig. Buckett strips off the Pieman's outfit to reveal his own clothes underneath

Spade (*chuckling*) Here. It worked. Just like the Knave said it would.
Buckett Course it did. (*He glances off*) And now for the second part of the plan. Here comes the *real* Pieman.

Buckett hides the outfit behind his back and both men move away from the tray

The Pieman enters and crosses to the tray

Pieman (*about to pick it up*) What? Only *two* pigs left. I'm sure there were three.
Buckett That's right, Guv. There were. One, two, three.
Pieman Then where's the other one?
Spade The man took it, didn't he? Just a few seconds ago.
Pieman What man? And where's his penny?
Buckett Oh, he didn't leave no penny. He just took the pig and ran off.
Pieman (*aghast*) You mean he *stole* it?
Spade We certainly do. We tried to stop him, too, didn't we, Buckett?
Buckett I'll say. But he was too quick for us.

Pieman (*horrified*) Oh, no. (*Calling loudly*) Help. Help.

Kitty, Jack and the Choristers come hurrying on

Crowd What is it? What's happening? Etc.

Jack (*stepping forward*) What seems to be the trouble, Mr Pieman?

Pieman Somebody's stolen one of my pigs, and these two saw him do it.

Everyone reacts with horror and consternation

Jack (*to them*) Who was it?

Buckett (*pointing off*) Him over there. The one that's running.

Kitty (*looking*) But that's Tom Sprightly. You're not trying to tell us that *he* stole it?

Jack Absolute rubbish. I don't believe a word of it.

Spade All right, then. You chase after him and see. He was eating it as he left here.

Jack (*grimly*) Very well. But I just hope for your sakes that you're telling the truth, because if you aren't . . . (*To the others*) Come on, everybody. After him.

With loud cries of "Stop thief!", all hurry off in pursuit

Buckett and Spade are left behind, chortling, and the Lights fade quickly to Black-out

SCENE 4

Another part of the Fayre

The Lights come up to full on a lane cloth depicting the exterior of a large tent, or animal cages on wheels

Dame Sprightly enters with a few bundles of sticks

Dame (*calling weakly*) Firewood for sale. Firewood for sale. (*To the audience*) Oh, boys and girls, whatever am I going to do? I haven't sold one bundle of firewood yet, and the Fayre's half over. I do hope my Tom's having a bit better luck. (*She glances down*) Oh. (*She drops her sticks and picks up a pound note from the floor*) A pound note. I've found a pound note. (*Wisely*) I'd better take it along to the police station, hadn't I? They might be offering a five-pound reward for finding it.

The Chamberlain enters L

Chamberlain (*relieved*) Oh. Dame Sprightly. The very person I'm looking for. You owe me two pounds and I need it rather urgently.

Dame Ooo-er. I'd forgotten all about it.

Chamberlain Oh, dear. I thought you may have done, but it *is* very pressing. So if you wouldn't mind . . . (*He holds out his hand for the money*)

Dame (*worried*) But I haven't got it. I mean, this pound note's the only bit of money I've touched in days. (*She shows the note*)

Chamberlain (*beaming*) Well, that's *half* of it, isn't it? I'll tell you what. I'll take this one for the moment, and you can give me the other one later. (*He takes it*) Many thanks. (*He turns to exit the way he came*)

Georgie enters L.

Georgie (*to the audience*) Hiya, kids. (*To the Chamberlain*) Oh, Mr Chamberlain. The very person I'm looking for. You owe me two pounds for cleaning up the silverware for you. Can I have it? I want to buy some sweets for the kiddies. (*He holds out his hand*)

Chamberlain (*taken aback*) Oh—well—er ... As a matter of fact, I haven't got two pounds on me. This pound note is all the money I'm carrying.

Georgie (*cheerfully*) That's all right. I'll take that for the moment, and you can give me the other one later. (*He takes it and begins to exit*) Ta.

Dame (*quickly*) Here, Georgie. Before you go rushing off, what about the two pounds *you* owe *me*?

Georgie (*wincing*) Oh, heck. You don't want it right now, do you? I've only got this one. (*He shows it*)

Dame Never mind. You can give me that and pay me the rest in a minute. (*She takes the note from him. To the Chamberlain*) Now then. Here's the pound I owe you. (*She gives it to him*) So that makes *us* straight.

Chamberlain (*to Georgie*) And here's the pound *I* owe *you*. (*He gives it to him*) So that makes *us* straight.

Dame (*snatching the note from Georgie*) And this is the pound *you* owed *me*, so that makes *us* straight. (*She slips it down the front of her dress*) And this goes right down here. (*She manoeuvres her bust*) And that's them straight. (*She smiles sweetly at the men*) Bye-bye, boys.

The Chamberlain and Georgie exit L, *bewildered*

Dame Sprightly moves to pick up her sticks

Tom enters R, *holding half the pastry pig*

Tom (*cheerfully*) Hi, Mum.

Dame I know. It's the heels on these shoes that do it. (*She notices Tom's pig*) What's that you're eating?

Tom A pastry pig. It's absolutely delicious. Here (*he offers it*) I've saved half for you.

Dame (*annoyed*) You've not been spending our firewood money on pastry pigs, have you? You naughty, good-for-nothing, young——

Tom Calm down, Mum, calm down. It didn't cost me a penny. The Pieman was giving them away. Just for today.

Dame (*startled*) You what? You mean giving them away for nothing? Without charge? Free, gratis, and honi saki mouldy fence?

Tom That's right. (*He offers the pig again*)

Dame (*grabbing it and taking a bite*) Ohhhhhh. And to think I've spent my pension money on a few slices of tongue for the supper. We could have filled up on pastry pigs instead. (*She finishes chewing*)

Tom (*dismayed*) We're not having *tongue* for supper, Mum.

Dame Why not? It's very tasty, tongue is. What's wrong with it?

Tom Well nothing. I suppose, but I couldn't eat *anything* that's come out of animal's mouth. (*He shudders*)

Dame Oh, all right. You can have an egg. Now let's get these sticks picked up and see if we can sell some. (*She picks up the bundles*)

Tom You don't have to worry about selling sticks any more, Mum. In a few minutes' time, you're in for the surprise of your life.

Dame Yes. That's what your father said when your grandad sat down on the circular saw.

Jack, Kitty, the Pieman and some Villagers enter

Pieman (*pointing at Tom*) There he is. Grab him.

The Villagers rush over to Tom and sieze him

Tom (*bewildered*) What's wrong? What is it?

Dame (*startled*) Help. Fire. Police.

Kitty (*concerned*) Did you take a pie from the Pieman's tray, Tom?

Tom (*puzzled*) Why, yes. Of course I did. We've just eaten it.

Jack (*sorrowfully*) Then I'm afraid I've got to arrest you on a charge of theft.

Tom }
Dame } (*together*) What? (*They exchange bewildered glances*)

Pieman To the royal pavilion with him.

The angry Villagers begin to drag Tom off

Tom (*struggling*) No. Wait ...

Crowd (*beating at him*) Thief. Villain. Etc.

Bewildered and protesting. Tom is dragged off by the Villagers. All follow, with Jack and Kitty comforting Dame Sprightly

The Lights fade quickly to Black-out

SCENE 5

Inside the Royal Pavilion

The Lights come up on a large hall with twin thrones set on a dais far L, angled towards the audience R

King Cole and Queen Mattiwilda are leading their guests in a merry, whirling dance

SONG 8

At the end of the number, everyone applauds breathlessly, then withdraws to the outer limits of the area to chat silently, leaving the King and Queen alone down C

Queen (*contentedly*) Oh, Aloysius, wasn't that wonderful? I do declare, my feet scarcely seemed to touch the ground.

King You're perfectly right, my dear. Most of the time they were on top of mine. (*He winces*)

The Herald enters R

Herald (*announcing*) Her Royal Highness, the Princess Marigold.

The Princess enters in a fresh gown

The guests all defer to her and she moves to her parents

The Herald exits

King (*beaming at her*) Ah, there you are, my sweet. We were wondering where you'd got to.

Princess (*embracing him*) Oh, Father. I've had the most wonderful time today.

King Have you, dear? That's good. Your mother and I have been enjoying ourselves, too.

Queen (*pecking Marigold on the cheek*) Yes. We've been trying out everything in the Fayreground. Everything from the Ghost Train to the Tunnel of Love.

Princess (*amused*) The Tunnel of Love? You two?

Queen Why not? Mind you, I can't say we particularly *enjoyed* it. I mean, the scenery was pretty and we loved the way the coloured lights reflected on the water, but we both got *soaking wet.*

Princess (*concerned*) Don't tell me your boat sprang a leak?

King (*blankly*) Boat? What boat?

The Princess laughs delightedly

Anyway, after we'd dried out, I went on one of those ingenious old-fashioned weighing machines. You know, the type that *tells* your fortune as well as giving you your weight.

Queen Yes. It was absolutely fascinating. Look. I've got his card right here. (*She gets out a small pasteboard card and shows it*) It says: (*reading*) "You are handsome, virile, oozing with charm and personality, and have above average intelligence."

The King looks smug as the list is read out

It even got his *weight* wrong. (*She chuckles*)

King (*embarrassed*) Harumph. Never mind about that, Matti. It was nothing important. (*He clears his throat loudly, then speaks to Marigold*) And what is it *you've* been up to, my poppet?

Princess Well—promise you won't be cross if I tell you?

The King and Queen exchange fond glances

As a matter of fact (*she moves* L *in front of them*) I ran away from the Lord Chamberlain again and met the most exciting young man I've ever seen in my whole life. (*She turns to face them*)

Queen (*moving down to her*) Good heavens. It's not (*names a well-known pop singer*), is it?

Princess (*laughing*) No, no, Mother. *This* young man is far nicer than him. And what's more he can play the pipes. (*To the King*) Oh, Father, you will give him a job at the palace, won't you? I promised him you would.

King (*embarrassed again*) Oh . . . Well . . . I—er—er . . .
Princess (*pleading*) *Please.*

The Chamberlain enters in great distress

Chamberlain Your Majesties. Your Majesties. (*He hurries over to them*)

All turn to see what the commotion is about

Oh, however am I going to tell you? (*Anguished*) I've just heard the most
terrible news.
Queen Oh, no. (*Names local football team*) haven't lost again?
Chamberlain No, no, Your Majesty. Someone's committed a *crime.*

Everyone reacts in horror

King But—but that's *impossible.* I mean, they wouldn't *dare.* (*Very worried*)
Oh, dear. I knew it. I knew it would happen sooner or later. (*Accusingly*)
Somebody's shot the Prime Minister, haven't they?
Chamberlain (*taken aback*) Shot the Prime Minister? (*Recovering*) No, no,
sire. Of course they haven't.
King (*groaning*) Then it *is* true. Someone *has* committed a crime.
Chamberlain Oh, do be serious, Your Majesty. We could all be in terrible
danger.
Queen He's quite right, Aloysius. If a crime has been committed and the spell
is broken, this could mean the end of civilization as we know it. By this time
next week, we could all be forced to watch (*names a poor-quality TV show*).

Everyone trembles with fright

King Ooo-er. I hadn't thought of that. We'd better investigate at once. (*To
the Chamberlain*) Well, don't just stand there quivering, man. Call out the
guards. Arrest the suspect immediately.
Chamberlain It's already been done, Your Majesty. The Foreman of the
Fayre detained him, and even now the villain is outside the hall, awaiting
your royal pleasure.
King (*annoyed*) I'll give him pleasure. Have him brought in right away.

The Chamberlain hurries off

*The King and Queen take their seats on the thrones and the Princess stands
beside the Queen*

Tom enters, escorted by two Soldiers. Jack and the Pieman follow

Princess (*recognizing him*) Tom.
King (*surprised*) Tom? Do you *know* this—this *person*, Marigold?
Princess It's the boy I've just been telling you about. Oh, Father, there must
be some mistake. Tom wouldn't commit a crime. I just know he wouldn't.
Pieman I'm sorry, Princess, but we caught him red-handed. The little thief
stole a pig from under my very nose, the moment I had my back turned.
Tom (*earnestly*) It's not true, Marigold. I swear it isn't.
King (*grimly*) Well, Master Horner?
Jack (*unhappily*) He'd certainly just finished eating a pig when we caught up

with him, Your Majesty, and he *did* admit to taking it from the Pieman's tray. But I can't understand it. Tom's no thief. I've known him all my life.

Pieman In that case what's happened to the money? A penny each, those pigs cost.

Tom But I keep trying to tell you. The *other* Pieman said they were free. He was giving them away just for today (*To the audience*) Wasn't he, boys and girls?

Audience reaction

Pieman (*scornfully*) Free pigs, indeed. A likely story. And what other Pieman's this? *I'm* the only Pieman at the Fayre today. Isn't that so, Mr Foreman?

Jack (*quietly*) I'm afraid so.

King (*standing*) Then there's no doubt about it. The boy is obviously guilty.

Tom No.

King Have you anything to say before I pass sentence, you wretched little juvenile detergent?

Tom Only that I'm innocent, Your Majesty. (*In despair*) Oh, why doesn't someone believe me?

Princess *I* believe you, Tom. Honestly, I do.

Jack And I'd *like* to.

Pieman It's no use, Princess. There were even witnesses who saw him take it.

Queen Witnesses? (*She rises*) Oh, then we must question them at once. (*To the Princess*) Don't worry, my dear. I know all about questioning witnesses. Why, I once appeared as a witness myself. In a very famous forgery trial.

King Yes, my sweet. But by the time *you'd* finished giving evidence, the jury were so confused, they sent the *judge* to jail. Never mind about the witnesses. The case has already been proved. (*To Tom*) Thanks to you, our pretty little kingdom has lost its magic protection and from now on we'll be at the mercy of anyone who cares to attack us. For this great crime, we sentence you to be beaten black and blue, then banished from the country for the rest of your life.

Tom looks dismayed

Princess No, Father. No.

King (*to the Soldiers*) Take him away.

Before the Soldiers can move, Kitty, Georgie and Dame Sprightly hurry in. Kitty and Georgie carry bundles of clothing

Kitty (*urgently*) Wait. Wait. Your Majesty. Look what we found behind one of the tents. (*She holds up the Pieman's costume and displays it*)

Pieman A pieman's outfit.

Georgie And these schoolboy clothes. (*He holds them up*)

Dame And guess who was seen hiding them there? Those two strangers who were wandering around the Fayre all afternoon.

Jack (*delightedly*) Then Tom's been telling us the truth all along. He *didn't* steal the pig. That pair of crooks were responsible for the whole thing. (*To Tom*) Oh, Tom. Can you ever forgive me for arresting you?

Tom (*relieved*) Of course I can. And I do. I suppose things *did* look bad. Thank goodness those outfits turned up in time, though.

Queen (*beaming*) So that means the spell's still working for us, doesn't it? We haven't had a crime after all?

King No. But we *nearly* did. If Mistress Fisher and her friends hadn't found these clothes, an innocent person would have been punished and *I'd* have committed one. (*Fuming*) Oooh. Just wait till I get my hands on those scoundrels. (*To the Soldiers*) Release this poor boy at once, and tell the Chamberlain to give him a bag of gold.

The Soldiers release Tom, and exit

Tom I don't want gold, Your Majesty. Just a chance to work here in the palace and earn an honest living.

King Permission granted.

The Princess hurries to Tom's side to congratulate him

Dame (*to the audience*) Oooh, doesn't it bring a lump to your throats?

There is the sound of harsh laughter, off, and the Knave of Hearts enters UL, followed by Buckett and Spade

Everyone reacts. The Knave swaggers down C. Buckett and Spade remain in the background

Queen (*startled*) Good heavens. It's pilfering Percy, the pop-eyed pastry pincher.

Knave (*sneering*) Greetings, Your Royal Highnesses. (*He bows mockingly*)

King (*outraged*) How *dare* you return to Nursery-rhyme Land without our royal permission?

Knave *Your* permission? (*He laughs*) I don't need *your* permission, you doddering old dunderhead. The Knave of Hearts goes where he pleases.

King Does he, indeed? We'll see about that. (*Calling*) Chamberlain.

Queen (*to the Knave*) Leave this pavilion at once, or we'll have you thrown into chains.

Knave Bah. You don't frighten *me*, you old has-been.

Dame I'm not surprised. If you're used to looking at *that* face in your shaving mirror every morning, nothing could frighten you.

Knave (*whirling round to face her*) Silence, you flannel-faced old faggot.

The Chamberlain enters, sees the Knave and reacts

Georgie Here, less of the name calling, you. That's a lady you're talking to, not your mother.

Knave (*glaring*) One more word from *you*, and I'll have your tongue cut out and fed to the palace dogs.

Chamberlain (*indignantly*) Over my dead body. They only eat Kennomeat.

Princess (*to the Knave*) Go away, you horrible looking man. Don't you know we're under the protection of the Fairy Queen?

Knave (*advancing on her with a leer*) You mean you *were*, my pretty poppet.

The Knave attempts to caress the Princess's face, but she avoids him

From the moment that pig was stolen the spell ended, and, as of now, the kingdom is mine and everyone in it, *my slave*. (*He laughs harshly*)

Tom Not so fast. Master Knave. No pig *was* stolen. The only crime committed by *those* two villains lurking behind you (*he indicates Buckett and Spade*) and as they don't belong in Nursery-rhyme Land, I think you'll find our protection just as good as ever it's been.

Knave (*sneering*) Indeed? Then tell me: which of you paid the Pieman for his pastry?

Jack (*realizing*) He's right. Until the Pieman's been paid, a crime has taken place.

Kitty Quick. Someone pay him his penny.

There is a frantic searching of pockets

Knave (*triumphantly*) Too late.

The Knave raises his arms quickly and casts a spell. There is a crash of thunder. The Lights flicker madly

The Pieman is suddenly swept away as though by a great wind

The guests cry out in fear and everyone huddles together

At last. At last. At long, long, last, my plans, ripe fruits have born.
The magic spell is shattered. Its protective cloak is torn.
From henceforth, I, the Knave of Hearts, shall wield the rod of power,
And all to *me* will bend the knee, whilst Fairyland doth cower.

Fairy Harmony enters

Fairy   Not so. For though by trickery, you seem to win the day,
There's many a slip twixt cup and lip, so hark to what I say.
The blameless youth you used to help you break our fairy spell,
Shall be the cause of *your* downfall. (*To Buckett and Spade*)
And yours, and yours as well. (*She turns back to the Knave*)
No matter if the Crown of Hearts sits square above your face,
Though King and Queen be in your hands,
With *my* help, Tom shall play the *Ace*.

Knave (*snarling*) Bah. You mealy-mouthed little munchkin. You can't stop me now. As soon as the crown is mine. I'll get rid of Master Tom once and for all. (*He laughs*)

Fairy Begone. (*She waves her wand*)

A white light falls on the Knave, who reels and staggers back. Buckett and Spade rush forward to assist him

Knave (*pushing them off*) For the moment your powers are strong, Harmony, but even now, they are failing. Soon you shall feel the full force of my Black Magic and I'll return to claim the crown as mine. (*To Buckett and Spade*) Come.

The Knave, Buckett and Spade exit. The white light goes out

Queen (*to the Fairy; relieved*) Oh, thank goodness you came in time, Harmony, dear. I do declare that man has improved worse with age. Do you know, he looked at me as though *I* were a dirty kitchen floor and he was a packet of Flash.

King (*anxiously*) He can't *really* take my crown, can he? Not *really*?

Fairy (*gently*) I'm afraid he can. And will. Without the spell to keep you safe, there's no end to the trouble he can cause.

Princess But the couldn't the Fairy Queen *restore* the spell for us? After all, it was broken by a trick and had nothing to do with us.

Fairy If only it were that simple. But you see, Princess, as soon as the fairy spell was broken, the Knave was able to cast one of his own. Every moment its power greatens, and even now, it's far too late for our Queen to help you.

Jack Then how is Tom able to help us?

Kitty (*to the Fairy*) You said *he'd* defeat the Knave. We heard you.

Fairy There is one chance still. At the end of the world is a strange island. A place of great danger where dreadful creatures lie in wait to devour the unwary.

Georgie Blimey. Sounds like the TUC Headquarters.

Dame Sprightly pushes him in indignation

Fairy At the very centre of this island, is an ancient tree known as the Tree of Truth, and in its branches, the long lost sword of the great King Arthur is hidden. If this can be wrested from beneath the eyes of its ever-watchful guardian, Nursery-rhyme Land can be saved. If not, the Knave of Hearts will rule forever.

Tom (*firmly*) Then show me the way, good Fairy. Guardian or no guardian, no black-hearted villain is going to rule *my* country. I'll get the sword.

Dame (*with tears in her eyes*) Oooh, isn't he brave, everybody? Can't you tell he takes after his dear old dad?

Chamberlain In what way, Dame Sprightly?

Dame (*proudly*) I'll tell you in what way. That boy's father was right there in the front line when the first shot of World War I was fired. (*Thoughtfully*) Mind you, when they fired the *second* one, he was back at home, hiding under the bed.

Fairy (*with wand raised*)
> Begin your quest, brave Piper's son, if wrongs you'd right in time.
> The Knave of Hearts will soon return to claim the throne of Nursery-rhyme.
> And though dark danger threatens you, let courage be your guide,
> I'll do my best to keep you safe, and be forever by your side.

Fairy Harmony exits

Tom (*firmly*) Right, Master Knave. You made a big mistake when you tried to get *me* branded as a thief, and before very long, you're going to rue the day you were born. (*To the King and Queen*) Don't worry, Your

Majesties. He may have the upper hand at the moment, but I swear I'll return with the magic sword before you can say Jack Robinson.

Princess Oh, Tom. Do be careful.

Tom I will, Marigold. (*To the King*) And now, Your Majesty, I ask but for three things. A cloak, a sword, and everyone's good wishes to cheer me on my way.

King Chamberlain.

The Chamberlain signals

Two Page-boys enter with a cloak and a sword on a velvet cushion

Tom puts on the cloak and takes the sword

Dame And don't forget to put clean underwear on. You never know when you're going to be knocked down and taken to hospital.

Tom (*smiling*) All right, Mum. (*Raising the sword high*) To the island at the end of the world, and the Tree of truth.

SONG 9

This is sung first by Tom as a solo, then Principals and Choristers join in the reprise for a big finale to Act I. At the end of the song———

———the CURTAIN *falls*

ACT II

On the Quayside

A quaint old seaport. The backdrop depicts the harbour, sea-wall, assorted galleons and clipperships, distant cliffs and the sea. DR, is the local inn, which has a practical door, and L, is a collection of fishermen's cottages

When the Curtain rises, it is daylight and Sailors, in an assortment of costumes, are performing a cheerful, traditional hornpipe. This may be followed by a short selection of sea shanties, or a routine by the Children in miniaturized versions of the sailor's costumes

SONG 10

At the end of the song/routine, all exit variously and in character. As they do so, Tom and Jack enter UL, and move down C

Jack I wish you'd let me come with you, Tom. It would be the least I could do to make up for what happened yesterday.

Tom (*smiling*) Thanks, Jack, but I'll be a lot happier knowing you stayed behind to look after the others. When the Knave finds out where I've gone and what I'm trying to do, he's bound to try and stop me. Who knows, he might try to do it by threatening to harm *them*. Just keep them out of his way till I get back with the magic sword. *Then* we'll see how tough he really is.

Jack (*disappointedly*) All right. But I still wouldn't have minded crossing swords with whatever creatures you're going to find on this mysterious island. There's nothing I like better than a good fight, be they ghosts, ghouls or goblins.

Tom (*shaking Jack's hand*) Well, I'd better be off. I've still got to find the *Jolly Mermaid* and pay the Captain for my passage. (*He glances off* UR) Ah, here he comes now.

The Ship's Captain enters, frowning

Good-morning, Captain.

Captain Arr. (*His eyes dart suspiciously around the quayside*)

Tom You—er—you seem a trifle worried. Is something wrong?

Captain Arr. I seem to have lost a few of my crew, the scurvy dogs. They wuz all here at first light, but since them soldiers posted that notice on the board over yonder (*he indicates off*), they seems to have vanished.

Tom (*curious*) What does it say?

Captain (*quoting*) "Under pain of death, no ship or sailor is to leave port without permission of our new ruler—the Knave of Hearts."

Jack (*dismayed*) Oh, no. (*To Tom*) How are you going to get to the island now?

Captain Don't worry, me fine bucko. As far as *I'm* concerned, King Cole and Queen Mattiwilda are still in charge of Nursery-rhyme Land, and no mutineering Knave is going to give *me* orders. The *Jolly Mermaid* sails within the hour.

Tom But how can she? I mean, you said you hadn't a crew.

Captain (*winking*) You leave that to me. There'll be a full crew on board before we sails, I promise yer. Go stow your luggage and I'll meet yer on board in two shakes of a lamb's tail. There's a little business I have to attend to in here.

The Captain exits into the inn

Tom Well, cheerio, Jack. I'll see you when I return. (*He begins to move off*)

Jack Wait. I'll come and wave you off. That way I'll know you got away safely.

Jack follows Tom off UL. *As they exit, Buckett and Spade enter* DR, *in a furtive manner*

Buckett What did I tell you? I knew those two were up to something the minute we saw them sneaking out of the back entrance to the palace. Did you hear them? That Piper's son is going to leave port without asking permission. (*Chortling*) Just wait till the boss hears about *this*. (*He rubs his hands together with glee*)

Spade (*uncomfortably*) Do we *have* to tell him, Buckett?

Buckett (*amazed*) You *what?* Of *course* we have to tell him. How else do you think we're going to get paid?

Spade I'm not so sure I want to get paid, now. I keep thinking about the funny look that Fairy gave me.

Buckett (*sneering*) Give over. She didn't give you that. You've always had it. Listen. Forget the Fairy. She can't do a thing to us now that old grisly features rules the place. All we have to do is keep *him* happy, and we've got a job for life.

Spade Yes. But what if we upset him one day? You know how bad-tempered he gets when something goes wrong. (*Glumly*) He's such a pain in the neck, the Ralgex people are going to give him a royalty.

Buckett Here, and talking about royalty: who's keeping an eye on the King and Queen, and that pretty little Princess Marigold?

Spade Don't ask me. Perhaps they're locked up in the Tower like Anne Boleyn.

Buckett Anne *who?*

Spade Anne Boleyn. (*Curiously*) You have heard of Anne Boleyn?

Buckett (*blustering*) Course I have. Everybody's heard of Anne *Boleyn*.

Spade All right, then, who was she?

Buckett (*jeering*) Ahhhhh, you can't catch *me* out. Anne Boleyn wasn't a *she*, Anne Boleyn was a steam iron. (*He nods smugly*)

Spade (*puzzled*) How do you work that out?

Buckett It's in all the history books, isn't it? (*He quotes*) When Henry the Eighth finally got rid of his *first* wife, he lost no time in pressing his suit with Anne Boleyn. (*He mimes ironing a suit*)

Spade (*wincing*) Ooh, if Moses had known about you, he'd have gone back for another commandment. Anyway, what are we going to do about this ship? You heard what the Captain said. He's going to be sailing within the hour. By the time we get back to the palace and tell the Knave, it'll have gone.

Buckett Yes. You're right. (*He thinks quickly*) There's only one thing for it. We'll have to sneak on board and find somewhere to hide. Once we're at sea, we can creep up on young Master Tom, throw him over the side, then force the Captain to bring us back to shore again. Come on.

Buckett and Spade exit UR. *As they do so, the Captain enters from the inn with several rough-looking sailors*

Captain Now ye're absolutely clear? I needs as many extra crew as yer can find—includin' a good cook. An' I ain't too particular as to how yer get's 'em. (*He hands over a bag of gold*)

The Captain exits UR

Sailor Right, lads. You know what we're looking for.

The Sailors exit variously. As they do so, Dame Sprightly and Georgie enter DL. *Both are dressed in outlandish sailor costumes*

Georgie (*to the audience*) Hiya, kids.

Dame (*sharply*) Shhhh. We're supposed to be in disguise. You haven't to let people reconciliate you. (*She pulls him closer*) Now listen. We've got to find some way of getting on board our Tom's ship without anybody spotting us. I'm not having him sailing into danger on his own. He's going to be protected whether he likes it or not.

Georgie Well how are we going to manage that? You can't just walk on to a boat, you know.

Dame (*wisely*) You leave it to me. I know all about boats, I do. My late husband was a sailor.

Georgie Eh? (*He looks at her in bewilderment*)

Dame (*grudgingly*) Well ... not *exactly* a sailor. He used to lead a horse pulling a barge down the canals—but it's close enough.

Georgie And what do you think we're going to do if we *do* manage to get aboard? I mean, look at us. I'm as nervous as a long-tailed cat in a room full of rocking chairs, and you're just a broken-down, wrinkled, half-senile old woman.

Dame (*outraged*) I *beg* your pardon? Don't you ever call me old again. (*Huffily*) I might not be in the first flush of youth any more, but I've still got a *few* fellers chasing after me. (*She preens*) As a matter of fact, only last week I had to say "No" to quite a number of them.

Georgie Why? Didn't you like what they were selling?

Dame (*put out*) Ooooh. That's typical of you, that is. Think you're the only man in a young girl's life. Well for your inflammation, you're not. (*Smugly*) The Lord Chancellor's got his eye on *me*.

Georgie Old Neville? How do you work *that* out?

Dame (*off-handedly*) Simple. Every time he speaks to me, he calls me "Fair Lady". (*She simpers*)

Georgie Oh, that's just force of habit. He used to be a bus conductor. (*He chortles with laughter*)

Dame (*tartly*) Har, har. Very funny. (*Sweetly*) But I'm glad you mentioned conducting, because that's reminded me about our wedding.

Georgie (*startled*) Eh?

Dame Yes. Bus conductors ring bells, and bells are what I'm waiting to hear. Wedding bells. (*Sharply*) As soon as we get back from this voyage, I want to see a ring on this finger. (*She indicates it*)

Georgie What happened to the last one I gave to you? The lucky gold one I got from that gypsy?

Dame I had to throw it away. I only wore it two days and my finger went green.

Georgie Oh. I'm sorry about that, Aubergine, but not to worry. (*He shrugs*) I wasn't going to give it to you till we got back, but ... well ... I bought you a new ring only this morning. Look. (*He gets a large diamond ring out of his pocket and shows it to her*)

Dame (*grabbing it eagerly*) Ooooooh. A diamond engagement ring. (*To the audience*) Oh, girls, girls. I've managed it at last. We're going to be joined in holy deadlock. (*She gazes at the ring*) A diamond engagem——(*She stops and peers at it more closely*) Here, are you *sure* this is a diamond?

Georgie Well if it isn't, I've been diddled out of twenty p.

Dame (*to the audience*) Bless his little heart. He's the salt of the earth, isn't he? (*Grimly*) I think I'll stick him in a cellar. (*To him*) Listen, loppy lugs, if you think I'm going to put that thing on *my* finger, you've got another think coming. That's an Irish diamond, that is.

Georgie (*blankly*) Irish diamond?

Dame Yes. A sham rock. I'd only have to drop it once and I'd get seven years' bad luck. (*Annoyed*) Ooooh, you're so tight-fisted, if you found a packet of corn plasters, you'd start wearing tight shoes.

Georgie (*embarrassed*) Oh, give over.

Dame You wouldn't even get into a fight unless it was a *free*-for-all. (*To the audience*) And to think that on his last birthday, I spent all my money on a present that made his eyes pop out.

Georgie Yes. A shirt with a collar five sizes too small.

She begins to sniffle

Oh, don't get upset, Aubergine. It was only a joke. Here, listen. Guess what I'm going to buy you for a wedding present. A lovely pearl necklace.

Dame Pearl necklace? I don't want a pearl necklace. I want a motor car.

Georgie Yes, I know. But I don't know where to buy imitation cars.

Dame Sprightly starts to cry loudly

Oh, don't cry. I was only pulling your leg. Honestly. Of course I'll get you a car. I'd do anything for *you*. You know that.

Dame (*sniffling*) I bet you would.

Georgie (*insistantly*) I would. If I had to, I'd even *die* for you.

Dame Yes. You keep saying that, but you never do it, do you?

Georgie (*coaxingly*) Come on. Give me a smile.

She gives a weak, forced smile

You can do better than that.

She gives him a huge grin

(*To the audience*) "Jaws Three." (*He beams at her*)

Dame Well, if we're going to be friends again, we'd better get on with what we're supposed to be doing. Finding a way of getting on board that ship.

Georgie Oh, do we have to, Aubergine? You know I'm scared of water. What'd happen if the ship went down? I can't swim and I'd drown.

Dame No you wouldn't. I'll give you a tablet of soap and it'll wash you back to shore. Come on.

Grabbing hold of his collar, Dame Sprightly drags Georgie off UR

The Lights dim

The Knave enters DL, *wearing the royal crown and laughing in triumph*

Knave (*grandly*) Behold. The new King of Nursery-rhyme Land. (*He leers at the audience to provoke a reaction*) Silence, you miserable rabble, or I'll shorten the school holidays. (*He smirks*) Now to inspect the royal fleet and choose a suitable ship for my purpose. Ex-King Cole and his idiotic wife will be taken out to sea and thrown to the sharks. (*He roars with laughter, then muses*) But what of Princess Marigold? She's far too tasty a dish to share *their* fate. (*Slyly*) Perhaps I can think up something *much* more delightful for *her*. (*He glances sharply off* UL) Why, here she comes now. I'll hide over yonder and see what she's up to.

The Knave exits quickly behind the inn

The Lights come up to full again

The Princess and Kitty enter UL

Kitty Here we are, Your Highness.

Princess (*anxiously*) Oh, I do hope we're in time, Kitty. I've just got to see him again before he leaves.

Kitty (*glancing off* UR) That looks like the *Jolly Mermaid* over there. (*She indicates*) Would you like me to go and see?

Princess If you wouldn't mind. But do be careful. Keep an eye out for the Knave's men, too. Since last night, his spies seem to be everywhere. (*Despondently*) Oh, Kitty. We've just got to get hold of that magic sword, or it's the end for us all.

Kitty Don't worry, Princess. If anyone can find it, Tom will. And with Fairy Harmony to help him, you can be sure that nasty Knave won't be ruling the country for very long.

Kitty exits UR

Princess (*moving down* C) If only we *could* be sure. (*She sighs*) Isn't it strange? Only yesterday I was longing for excitement and adventure, and now, here I am, wishing that everything were back to normal.

The Children enter DR. *They move to her*

Children Hello, Princess Marigold.
Princess (*brightening*) Why, hello. What are *you* doing here?
1st Child Trying to keep away from that horrible Knave. Everything's going wrong since *he* became King.
2nd Child Humpty Dumpty's fallen off the wall. Little Bo-Peep's lost *all* her sheep, and poor Miss Muffet's been frightened by an *enormous* spider.
3rd Child Even the village school's been closed down. (*Tearfully*) We don't like it here any more.
Princess (*kneeling to them*) Don't cry. It won't be like this forever, I promise. As soon as Tom gets back, we'll make everything right again.
4th Child (*brightening*) Honest and truly?
Princess Honest and truly.
5th Child *I* wouldn't mind if we didn't have to go back to school.
Princess (*surprised*) Oh. But you have to go to school (*names child*) You wouldn't like to grow up a *dunce*, would you?
6th Child But playing is *so* much more fun, Princess.
Princess Perhaps it is—at the moment. But unless you learn your lessons, you'll never learn how to do all the things that seem impossible to you now.
1st Child Like *what*?
Princess Well—like swinging on a star.

SONG 11

The Princess and Children sing

The Children exit DL *cheerily, at the end of the song, while the Knave moves out of hiding* DR

The Princess moves backwards DR, *waving off the Children. As the last one exits, she turns and collides with the Knave. The Lights dim*

(*Startled*) Oh . . .
Knave (*grabbing her*) So, my pretty little Princess. Your precious Tom is about to sail on the *Jolly Mermaid*, is he? (*He leers at her*)
Princess (*struggling*) Let me go.
Knave (*ignoring her*) Well, we shall see about that. He'll never lay hands on King Arthur's sword. Even with the help of that fool, Harmony, my powers will prove too strong for him. (*He pulls her* L) Come. To the royal palace and my Temple of the Black Art. (*He laughs harshly*)

Princess What are you going to do?

Knave Transport myself to the Enchanted Island and set a trap for *both* of them. (*He begins to drag her off*)

Princess (*struggling helplessly*) Help. Help.

The Knave and Princess exit

The Lights return to normal

King Cole enters in a furtive manner. He is dressed in shabby clothing and obviously disguised. He peers around, then signals off

King (*in a hoarse whisper*) It's all right, Mattie. The coast is clear.

The Queen enters similarly disguised

Queen Clear? You mean all the ships have gone? (*She peers anxiously about*)

King No, no. Of course they haven't. I simply mean that there's no-one around. Now if only we can find the royal yacht ... (*He looks about in bewilderment*) Oh, where's the Chamberlain? He'd know where it was at once.

Queen He's looking for Marigold, dear. We can't leave without *her*.

King (*despondently*) Oh, Matti, to think we've come down to this. Sneaking out of our own country like common criminals.

Queen Well, it won't be for long, dear. Let's just look at it as a nice little holiday.

King Holiday? With armed guards chasing us around, dogs snapping at our heels, strict curfews, and unthinkable tortures facing us if we're caught? What kind of a holiday is that?

Queen A Butlins one? Oh, don't be upset, Aloysius. We could always visit Athens and see those marvellous old ruins. Look. (*She gets a photograph out*) I got this photograph of it from (*names local travel agency*).

King (*taking it and looking*) Oh. Very nice.

Queen There's just one thing that puzzles me, though. If that's Athens, what's all that white stuff on top of the mountains?

King Well ... it's snow, isn't it?

Queen That's what I thought. But when I showed the picture to Marigold, *she* took one look at it and said it was Greece.

King (*handing the picture back*) Anyway, I don't want to go on holiday. I want my crown and country back. (*Annoyed*) Oooh, I *hate* that Knave of Hearts.

Queen (*soothingly*) Now, now, Aloysius. He probably can't help being the way he is. After all, he had a very unfortunate childhood. Don't you remember how his parents almost lost him?

King Yes, but they didn't take him far enough into the woods. They should have filled his sand-pit with quicksand.

The Chamberlain enters, breathlessly

Chamberlain Oh, Your Majesties. Calamity. I can't find the Princess anywhere, and the royal yacht is under guard. No-one's allowed to leave the harbour without the Knave's permission. Whatever are we going to do?

King (*drawing himself up*) *I'll* tell you what we're going to do.
Chamberlain (*eagerly*) Yes, sire?
King We're going to surrender. (*Dejectedly*) It's no use, Matti. We'll never get away now.

Jack and Kitty enter UR

Kitty (*urgently*) Princess. Quickly. The ship's about to set sail. (*Seeing the others*) Oh ...
Jack Your Majesties.

Jack and Kitty defer

King Oh, never mind about that. Is Marigold *here*?
Kitty She was a few minutes ago. (*She looks around anxiously*)
King (*agitatedly*) Then find her. Quickly. Perhaps we can all escape together.

The rough-looking Sailors enter

Sailor (*triumphantly*) Here's a likely-looking lot. (*He indicates them*)
Jack (*alarmed*) Look out. It's a press gang.
Queen Oh, good. I'll have the *Mirror*, *The Sun*, and *The Daily Express*.
Sailor Grab 'em.

The Sailors swoop on the party and carry them off with much commotion

The Lights fade quickly to Black-out and in the darkness a voice is heard

Voice (*off*) Weigh the anchor, ye swabs. Cast off.

SCENE 2

On board the "Jolly Mermaid"

The Lights come up to full on the ship's deck, with a view of the sea. If required, this can be played in front of the lane cloth, using the audience as the sea

If the Children were not used in the previous scene opening, a sailor routine may be interpolated here

SONG 11A (optional)

After the song/dance, the Children exit quickly. Buckett and Spade enter furtively L. *Spade is shivering violently*

Spade Ohhhhhh. How long are we going to be stuck on board this ship? I'm as cold as an icicle.
Buckett Oh, stop complaining. I found you a nice, private cabin, didn't I?
Spade Nice? What's nice about it? It's too small, freezing cold, and every time I close the door, the little light goes out.
Buckett (*grimacing*) You're never satisfied, are you? Never satisfied.
Spade (*defensively*) Well, we've been sailing for two weeks, and we still haven't managed to push that Tom character overboard.
Buckett Of course we haven't. It's no use doing it close to the shore. He

might swim to safety. No, we've got to wait for some really deep water. (*He rubs his hands together gleefully*)

Spade Yes, but what if the boss says he wants to see the spot where we did it?

Buckett Simple. After we've done the job, we put a great big chalk mark on the bottom of the boat to mark the spot. (*He smirks*)

Spade (*pushing him*) That's not going to work, you fathead. What happens if we come back on a different boat. Anyway, *I'm* not so sure that pushing him over the side is such a good idea. Remember last week when that solicitor chap fell overboard?

Buckett What about it?

Spade Well, *he* landed in the middle of all those sharks, didn't he? And not one of 'em went near him. They just cleared a path for him so he could climb back on to the ship.

Buckett Of course they did. That's what's known as professional courtesy.

The Captain enters

Captain Ahaaaaaa. Have either of you two swabs clapped eyes on a sailor with one leg, called Jackson?

Spade What do they call his other one? (*He chortles*)

Captain (*glowering*) Are you trying to be funny, bucko? (*He puts his hand to his cutlass*)

Spade (*gulping*) N-no, Captain. Certainly not.

Captain Then you're succeeding. (*Suspiciously*) Here, just a minute. I don't remember seeing you two before. Yer wouldn't be a couple of *stowaways*, would yer?

Buckett ⎱
Spade ⎰ (*together*) Us?

Captain (*menacingly*) Cause if you are . . . (*He draws his cutlass*) I'll have yer walking the plank. I hates stowaways.

Buckett (*giving a nervous laugh*) Oh, we're not stowaways. We—er—we work below deck, Captain. He's the ship's carpenter and I'm his mate.

Captain Ship's carpenter, eh? What are ye making at the moment?

Spade (*thrown*) Oh—er . . . I—er . . . I'm making a *portable*.

Captain Portable *what*?

Spade I don't know, Captain. I've only made the handles, so far.

Captain (*to the audience, aside*) There's somethin' fishy about this pair. I'll ask 'em a question that every seaman knows the answer to. (*To them*) I hears tell as how *Captain Cook* made *five* voyages, and on *one of 'em*, he was killed. (*Menacingly*) Which one was it?

Buckett (*gulping*) Couldn't you ask us another. We're not very good at history.

Captain (*loudly in triumph*) Stowaways. (*He waves his cutlass wildly*)

Buckett and Spade howl with fear and dash off L, *followed by the irate Captain. As they exit, Tom* R *enters*

Tom Not long now before we reach the Enchanted Island. If only I knew what to expect. (*He shrugs*) Well, I'll face that problem when I come to it. For the moment, I'm more concerned about Marigold and the others. I hope Jack's managed to keep them well hidden. The Knave's sure to have found out where I'm heading, by now. (*He glances off* R) Hello, *what's this?*

Two large cardboard boxes tiptoe on. Each is marked: NOT WANTED ON VOYAGE

(*Surprised*) Well, I've heard of a shifting cargo, but this is ridiculous. (*He quickly lifts up the first box to reveal Dame Sprightly*) Mother. (*He puts the box down*)

Dame (*flustered*) Oh ... fancy meeting you.

The second box is thrust off and Georgie appears

Georgie (*to the audience*) Hiya, kids.

Tom (*dazed*) How on earth did *you* get here?

Dame Shhhhhhh. We followed the ship's cat. He crept on board, but there wasn't a crypt in *this* craft, so we hurried to the hold and hid. (*She holds her stomach*) Oooh, you wouldn't have a ship's biscuit on you, by any chance, would you?

Georgie *I'd* settle for a dog's biscuit. We're absolutely starving.

Tom You mean you've had nothing to eat for two whole weeks?

Dame Well, I wouldn't say *that*. We did have two sacks of prunes and a few bottles of Mil-Par to keep us going.

Georgie Yes. And it did.

Tom But what are you doing on board the *Jolly Mermaid*? Don't you realize how annoyed the Captain's going to be if he finds you? He simply hates stowaways.

Georgie Pooh. You don't have to worry about *me*. I can look after myself. My dad happened to be a first-class boxer. (*He squares up his fists*)

Dame Yes, and your mother was a second-class poodle. (*To Tom*) Take no notice of him. Just treat him with ignoramus. *I'll* tell him what we're doing here. We've come to make sure that nothing happens to you. (*Beginning to sniffle*) After all, you're all I've got left, now. I don't know what I'd do if anything happened to take you away from me. (*She sobs*)

Tom (*comforting her*) Oh, Mum. Nothing's going to happen to me.

Dame (*blinking with surprise*) Isn't it? (*Annoyed*) Then what's the idea of doing *this* pantomime? We could have done *Aladdin*.

Voice (*loudly, off*) Land ho. Land ho.

Tom (*excitedly*) The island. It must be the island.

Dame Oh. Georgie. Quick. Back to the hold. We've got to get into our holiday clothes. (*To the audience*) Oh, girls. Just wait till you see my new outfit. The neckline plunges so deeply, you won't know if I'm trying to catch a man or bronchitis. (*She titters*)

Georgie (*indignantly*) Here. It's not that tiny little thing you were showing me a few minutes ago, is it? It's at least five sizes too small. Get yourself into that and it'll stop your circulation.

Dame No it won't. The tighter *my* clothes are, the more I circulate. (*She preens*)

Tom Speaking of clothes, I'd better go below and gather all *my* things together. We'll be landing before nightfall. See you later – and remember, don't let the Captain see you.

Tom exits R *quickly*

Georgie Come on, Aubergine. (*He picks up his box*)

Dame Just a minute. Just a minute. (*With feeling*) I want to remember this moment for the rest of my life.

Georgie Eh? (*He puts the box down again*)

Dame Well . . . Here we are, floating about on the high seas. Exotic perfumes wafting around us, carried on gentle breezes from a tropical island. And there's just you and me – (*she gives him a "come hither" look*) – with a full moon shining above.

Georgie Full moon? (*He looks around in bewilderment*) It's broad daylight.

There is a rapid dimming of the Lights, and a full moon is projected on to the lane cloth

Dame You were saying? (*Seductively*) Now why don't we play a nice little game? You pretend to be a poor sailor whose ship has just gone down in a terrible storm, and I'll be the girl who comes to save you: a beautiful, young, seductive, fascinating, golden-haired ravishing mermaid. (*She simpers*)

Georgie You what? (*He looks her up and down in amusement*) I'd never be able to pretend *that.* (*He chortles*)

Dame Of course you would. Anybody can pretend to be a *sailor.*

Georgie (*grinning*) All right, then. (*Cheerily*) Hey, missis. I'm looking for an old wreck that's sunk very low.

Dame Well, I'm here. (*She simpers, then realizes*) What do you mean, you're looking for an old wreck?

Georgie Oh, come on, Aubergine. Don't you think we're a bit old for playing daft games like that? (*Mockingly*) "You be a poor sailor, and I'll be a little mermaid."

Dame (*put out*) *I* don't see what's daft about it. The trouble with you is you've got no romance in your soul.

Georgie (*indignantly*) Yes I have. What about all those love letters I used to send you?

Dame (*snorting*) Some love letters. (*She gets one out and reads it*) "Dear Aubergine, I think of you all the time. Your naturally-waved hair, your brownish-grey eyes, those slightly prominent cheekbones and fresh complexion . . ." What's romantic about that?

Georgie Well, I sent you that from *work.* I used to write descriptions of missing people for the police.

Dame (*sniffling*) I don't know why I bother. (*She puts the letter away*) I might as well study to be a contortionist. Then at least I could sit down on my *own* knees. (*She sobs*)

Georgie Oh, don't start all that again. Look, as soon as we're on our way home again, I'll ask the Captain to marry us. How about *that* for being romantic?

Dame (*wide-eyed*) You mean we'll be married at sea by the Captain of this very ship?

Georgie Course not. We're not coming back on this old thing. It's only the very best for you. I've booked us a cabin on the *Titanic.*

SONG 12

George and Dame Sprightly sing

After the song, the Captain enters clutching his cutlass. He sees them and lets out a bellow of rage

Captain Stowaways! (*He waves the cutlass*)

With a yell of fear, Dame Sprightly and Georgie dash off pursued by the Captain

Black-out. In the darkness the two boxes are struck

SCENE 3

The Enchanted Island

A very spectacular scene of a tropical paradise. The backdrop is of rocky mountains, cascading streams and lush vegetation. Giant palm trees and floral shrubbery surround a clearing. If possible, all leaf edges should be sprinkled with gold or silver glitter to give a feeling of unreality. The area is bathed in dappled light, and a fallen tree or old log lies half in shadow

When the Lights come up, the Spirits of the Island are performing a graceful ballet. It is suggested that loosely flowing chiffons or gauzes can be used in costuming this to give a feeling of "flow". Solo dancers dressed as highly-coloured tropical birds can be added to this routine, but the whole thing should be as eye-catching as possible

SONG 13

As the dance ends, there is a flash and the Knave of Hearts appears with Princess Marigold in his grasp. She is now dressed in shabby clothing. Quickly and silently, the Spirits withdraw. The Birds give a squark of fright and vanish, leaving the Knave and Princess alone

Knave (*sneering*) Welcome to the island at the end of the world. Hiding place of the magic sword Excalibur, and home of Grendelgorm, its dreadful guardian. (*He laughs harshly*)
Princess (*pulling herself free*) Why bring *me* along, you revolting creature? I much prefer the company of the rats in the palace dungeons, to yours. (*She turns away from him*)
Knave (*leering*) Indeed? Then perhaps I'll have you returned there as soon as your purpose is fulfilled. (*He chuckles*)
Princess Purpose? (*She turns to face him*) What purpose?
Knave You shall see. With your assistance, I mean to make sure that Master Tom never crosses my path again. Not only will he fail in his quest, but his bones will be crushed in the mighty jaws of Grendelgorm and Nursery-rhyme Land shall be mine forever.
Princess Rubbish. I'll never help you. Never.

Knave You think not? Time will tell, my pretty Princess. Time will tell. Even now he approaches, led by that nauseous Fairy Harmony. (*He grabs her arm*) Come. To the Tree of Truth and the monster's lair. (*He begins to drag her off* L)

Princess (*struggling*) Tom. Help. Help.

With a harsh laugh, the Knave drags her off, but before they exit, she manages to drop her handkerchief

A moment later, Fairy Harmony enters UR, *followed by Tom, who now wears his cloak and carries his sword again*

Tom (*looking about him as he moves down* C) What an incredible place.

Fairy   Though beauty all around you lies, beware this isle of paradise.
Strange creatures long thought myth by man protect this place
Their lifelong span. And woe betide those reckless mortals
Who stray inside their mystic portals.

Tom I'll be careful, all right. But please, good Fairy, tell me something about this so-called guardian of the sword. Is he as frightening as you said?

Fairy   Indeed he is, and come the dawn, you'll meet the monster,
Grendelgorm:
A creature half as old as time, who only has one aim:
To kill unwary mortals if they enter his domain.
And though a thousand men have tried to get the best of *him*,
Alas, each valiant soul has died outside his cavern grim.

Tom (*bewildered*) Then what chance have I?

Fairy   The adversary you must fight, is the cruellest one on earth;
And ev'ry skill that you possess, you'll *need* to prove your worth.
He'll fight with all the power he has, to foil you in your quest,
But if your heart stays pure and true, you're sure to come out best.
(*She indicates off*)
Now rest your head in yonder bow'r, for comes the end of day.
The evening star will soon be out, and darkness hide the way.

Fairy Harmony exits

Tom (*calling*) Wait. Fairy Harmony. (*Disconcerted*) She's gone. (*He looks around*) Somehow this place doesn't look quite so attractive when you're on your own. There must be all sorts of strange creatures lurking in that undergrowth. Looks like I'll be sleeping with my sword at the ready, tonight. (*Seeing the handkerchief*) Hello, what's this? (*He picks it up*) A handkerchief. (*He examines it*) With the royal crest and Marigold's initials. (*Stunned*) But that's impossible. She's far away in England with Jack and the others . . . unless . . . (*Realizing*) Oh, no. The Knave must have captured her and brought her here to stop me getting the sword. I've got to find them.

He looks around helplessly, then hurries off DL

(*Calling as he goes*) Marigold. Where are you?

The King, Queen and Chamberlain enter UR. *They all look weary and carry baskets*

King (*groaning*) It's no use. I'll have to have a sit down. My bunions are killing me.

Chamberlain Couldn't you ask the court physician to do something for them, sire?

King (*wincing*) Why should I? They've never done much for *me*.

Queen (*looking into her basket*) We haven't gathered very many, have we?

Chamberlain (*dolefully*) I'm afraid not. We've scarcely covered the bottoms of the baskets.

King Bother the baskets. *I'm* not feeling well, and I'm sure we're all going to pick up some dreadful germs through landing on this island.

Chamberlain (*uneasily*) Oh, dear. (*Brightening*) Still, they do say that deep breathing will kill *any* kind of germ, don't they?

Queen Really? (*Curiously*) But how does one persuade them to breath deeply?

King (*wincing*) Matti . . . (*He sighs*) Fancy being reduced to *this*. Two weeks ago, ruler of Nursery-rhyme Land, and now, official collector of nuts and berries for a set of scruffy sailors.

Queen There, there. Don't upset yourself, dear. At least it's got us away from that terrible ship. It's the first time we've seen daylight since they kidnapped us.

Chamberlain How true. I've never been so humiliated in my entire life. Imagine. Me, the Court Chamberlain, washing dirty dishes in a ship's galley.

King (*indignantly*) And what about *us*? I had to scrub floors and peel vegetables, and poor Matti did all the cooking.

Queen (*shrugging*) That was nothing. As a matter of fact, I quite enjoyed myself. It's been *years* since I worked in a kitchen. Mind you, I wasn't always so good at cooking. (*She smiles at the King, fondly*) Remember the first meal I cooked after our wedding?

King I'll never forget it. Baked beans on toast.

Queen (*to the Chamberlain*) Yes. And it took me *six hours* to do it. The beans kept clogging up the toaster. (*She laughs lightly*) Then the following day I made a kipper and rhubarb casserole, but we never got the chance to eat it. A nasty burglar crept into the palace and scoffed the lot.

Chamberlain How unfortunate.

King Especially for him. His insurance policy just about covered his funeral expenses. But never mind about all that. We've got to find some way of escaping this place. Poor Marigold will be wondering where on earth we've got to.

Queen (*stricken*) Oh, my darling little girl. We might never see her again.

Chamberlain Don't worry, Your Majesty. All we have to do is hide until the ship sails, then wait to be rescued by friendly natives.

King Yes, but what if they expect us to *pay* them for doing it? We haven't a penny between us.

Chamberlain Fear not, Your Majesty. The solution's simple. *Everyone* knows that in out-of-the-way places like this, the natives use fish for money.

King *Fish?* You mean great slippery lumps of cod and haddock?

Chamberlain Exactly, sire.

Queen What a terrible time they must have trying to get chocolate bars out of slot machines.

King (*after a reaction*) Oh, very well, then. We'll give it a try. Where are we going to hide?

Chamberlain (*looking around hopefully*) There's bound to be a cave, or something close to hand.

Queen But what about Jack and Kitty? We can't leave *them* at the mercy of those nasty rough men.

King Quite right, Matti. We're all in this together. (*He thinks*) The only trouble is, how can we get to them? We haven't seen them since the ship left port.

Chamberlain Oh, but *I* have, Your Majesty. They were landing here as we were getting into the longboat. I think they're looking for fresh water.

King Splendid. Then off you go and find them.

Chamberlain (*gulping*) Me, sire? But – but – they could be on the other side of the island. And who knows what dreadful, ravenous beasts could be hiding amongst those trees? (*He looks at the trees fearfully*)

Queen Surely you're not afraid, Chamberlain? I thought you told me you were the son of a famous big-game hunter?

Chamberlain Oh, yes, Your Majesty. I am. When my father was in India, every night he'd go out shooting tigers.

King Every *night*?

Chamberlain Yes, sire. You see, when it's dark, their eyes blaze brightly, so all he had to do was wait till he saw a pair of blazing eyes, then shoot right between them. (*Proudly*) He was never known to miss.

Queen And where is he now?

Chamberlain Still in India. But *inside* a tiger. You see, after a while they realized what he was doing, and started to walk around in pairs with one eye shut. (*He winces*)

The King and Queen react

Jack and Kitty hurry into the clearing, carrying pails

Jack (*breathlessly*) Your Majesties, Lord Chamberlain. Thank goodness.

Kitty We've got the most marvellous news. That ship we were on was the *Jolly Mermaid*.

King (*startled*) But – but – that's the ship Master Sprightly was sailing on.

Jack That's right, sire. Which means that *this* place has to be the mysterious island of demons and monsters.

King (*nervously*) Oh, dear.

The King, Queen and Chamberlain exchange glances

Kitty And if it *is*, somewhere in the middle of it, Tom's searching for the magic sword. What a surprise he'll get when he finds out we're here, too.

King (*uneasily*) Yes.

Jack We'd better start looking for him before it really gets dark. There's no knowing how far we'll have to walk.

Chamberlain Er — couldn't we wait till morning? I mean — we — er — we don't want to get lost and bump into one of those monsters you were talking about, do we?

King Not to mention the snakes. Poor Matti almost trod on a couple of baby ones, a few moments ago.

Kitty Really? But how did you know they were baby ones, Your Majesty?

Queen Well, dear, they both had rattles.

Jack If you don't mind, Your Majesty, I'd rather we joined up with Tom before the morning. It'll be safer for all of us, and besides he's going to need all the help he can get.

King (*unhappily*) Oh, all right, then. Have it your own way. Which direction do we go in?

Chamberlain (*indicating* DL) Perhaps we should follow *that* path. It *might* lead us to him.

Queen (*smiling*) Don't be silly, Chamberlain. It won't lead us anywhere. We've been standing here for ages and it hasn't even *moved*.

Kitty All the same, someone *has* been this way recently. Look how the grass is trodden down.

Jack (*excitedly*) She's right. He must be just in front of us. Come on, everyone.

With much excitement, all exit DL. *One or two Spirits float quickly across the clearing, then Buckett and Spade enter breathlessly* R

Spade (*gasping for breath*) Oooh, I'm fed up with this lark. That Captain's been chasing us for miles. Fancy wanting us to walk the plank?

Buckett (*wheezing*) Yeah. He must have got out of his hammock on the wrong side of his cage. (*He looks round*) Here, I wonder where we are?

Spade Looks like the West Indies, to me.

Buckett *West Indies?* You wouldn't recognize the West Indies if they fell on you.

Spade Wouldn't I? I know everything about the West Indies, I do.

Buckett All right, then. What's their most famous product?

Spade Er — er . . . (*Weakly*) I don't know.

Buckett (*smugly*) Don't know. (*Patronizingly*) Where do you get *sugar* from?

Spade We borrow it from the woman next door.

Buckett pushes Spade in disgust

Dame Sprightly and Georgie hurry on

Georgie Hiya, kids. (*He sees Buckett and Spade*) Oh, look. How did *they* get here?

Dame (*advancing on them grimly*) I've no idea, but I *do* know how they're leaving. In a big wooden box. (*She squares her fists to them*)

Spade (*wearily*) Oh, don't *you* start on us, as well. We've had enough with that ship's Captain. Look at my ear. (*He displays it*) He scared me so much, I bit a chunk out of it.

Georgie Don't talk daft. How can anybody bite their own ear?

Spade (*weakly*) I was standing on a box.

Buckett Yeah, and when we jumped overboard to get away from him, *I* swallowed a frog.

Dame Ugh, I bet that made you feel sick.

Buckett It did. In fact, I thought for a minute I was going to croak.

Dame (*after a wince*) Anyway, what are you two doing here? I thought all dodos were extinct.

Spade (*uncomfortably*) Well, we stowed away, didn't we?

Georgie So did we. Here, and wasn't that Captain a bad-tempered old thing? He didn't half frighten us.

Dame Yes. But he didn't frighten me as much as *this* place does. Look how dark it's getting.

Buckett (*uneasily*) Here, she's right.

Dame (*looking around nervously*) I'm not very keen on the dark, either. Especially on islands that have monsters roaming around on 'em.

Buckett }
Spade } (*together*) Monsters?

Georgie Yes. The place is over-run with 'em.

Buckett }
Spade } (*together*) Ooo-er. (*They huddle together*)

Dame But there's no need to worry. I've just remembered. Monsters don't like music, so if we all sing at the top of our voices, perhaps it'll keep them away.

Georgie Good idea. What are we going to sing, then?

Buckett I know. "She was only the postman's daughter, but she knew how to handle the males."

Spade (*disgustedly*) That's no good. How about the war-time *meat-ration* song? "Whale meat again." I love Vera Lynn singing that.

Dame Oh, let's sing "Nellie Dean". We all know that.

Georgie Ah, but, what if we're singing and the monsters come up *behind* us?

Georgie Simple. All we have to do, is ask the girls and boys to let us know. (*To the audience*) Will you do that for us?

Georgie Will you?

Audience reaction, then the two villains bring down the log and all settle themselves on it, with Dame Sprightly and Georgie centre, and Buckett and Spade at each end. They begin to sing

After a moment a huge Gorilla enters

Audience reaction, by-play as required. When the song recommences, the Gorilla taps Buckett on the shoulder

Buckett turns and sees the Gorilla, shrieks with fright and dashes off, chased by the Gorilla

Dame (*looking round*) Here. Where's he dashing off to?

Georgie Perhaps he's gone to catch a bus.

Dame Don't be silly. He wouldn't have anywhere to keep it. Let's get on with the song.

They sing again

The Gorilla enters

He taps Spade on the shoulder who turns, then reacts

Spade rushes off madly

Georgie (*gazing after him*) Hey, the other one's gone now.
Dame Do you think it's something we've said? Still, never mind. It's much cosier without them, isn't it? I mean, now there's just the two of us.
Georgie (*uneasily*) Yes.
Dame (*pointedly*) Well?
Georgie Well, what?
Dame Are *you* going to start singing, or shall I?
Georgie Oh.

They begin to sing. Dame Sprightly snuggles up closer to him

The Gorilla enters and sits on the log next to Dame Sprightly

Dame (*pleasantly*) Hello. (*She continue singing, then reacts*)

Dame Sprightly jumps up and exits in a panic

Georgie continues singing. The Gorilla listens, then puts its arm around him. Without looking, Georgie rests his head on the Gorilla's chest. As the song ends, he slides down to rest his shoulders on the Gorilla's knees, and only then looks up to see its face

Georgie Oooh, Aubergine. You look really beautiful in this light. (*He flings his arms around the Gorilla's neck, and kisses the animal passionately*)

Suddenly Georgie realizes and with a yell, scrambles to his feet and dashes off. The Gorilla springs to its feet, clutches at its heart in a gesture of love, then sets off after him

Black-out. In the darkness the log is struck and the lane cloth brought in

SCENE 4

Another part of the Island

An evening light comes up on the lane cloth which depicts a dense jungle or forest

Tom enters R, still wearing the cloak and carrying sword

Tom (*despairingly*) It's no use. There's not a sign of them anywhere. Whatever am I going to do? (*He moves L*)

Fairy Harmony enters R

Fairy Don't worry, Tom. Though Marigold *is* the Knave's captive, she'll come to no harm. This I promise. Here on the Enchanted Island, my powers are still the equal of his. Be of good heart and not only will you rescue your princess, but Knave *and* Grendelgorm will fall to your sword. Take off your cloak.

Tom takes off his cloak and holds it out to her. She taps it with her wand

By virtue of my magic power — this cloak shall act in danger's hour
To keep you safe as safe can be. It's gift? Invisibility.

Tom You mean all I have to do is put it on and I'll be *invisible*? (*Delightedly*) Then how can I lose?

Fairy   (*sternly*) Beware of counting unborn chicks;
The Knave is full of cunning tricks.
He'll know you're there, by means of magic.
Take care, or die a death most tragic.

Fairy Harmony exits R

Tom (*ruefully*) She's right. I suppose I *was* getting a bit too sure of myself. (*He sighs*) It's just that deep down, I *do* feel scared about what's going to happen tomorrow. (*Earnestly*) Oh, Marigold, I know you can't hear me, but wherever you are, remember me in your prayers tonight. (*He sings*)

SONG 14

As the song comes to an end, the Lights fade to Black-out

SCENE 5

Outside Grendelgorm's Cave

There is a clearing with a backdrop of rocks, mountains and trees. A huge cave mouth is UL, *and* RC *stands a thick, overhanging tree with a fallen log at its base. This is the Tree of Truth. The sword Excalibur is fixed behind the tree (see the Author's Note on page vii). Rocks, trees and bushes hide all sightline gaps*

The Lights come up to give a daylight effect and the area outside the cavern is filled with Chefs and Serving-wenches. The Chefs hold wooden spoons or ladles, and the Serving-wenches have large trays of assorted foods on display. They are singing and dancing

SONG 15

At the end of the song, all march briskly into the cave. The Knave enters DL, *dragging Princess Marigold by the wrist*

Knave (*triumphantly*) Behold, the cave of Grendelgorm. (*He laughs and flings her* C) And now to bait my trap for Master Tom. (*Indicating the tree*) Upon that tree, the sword Excalibur hangs. Should anyone try to steal it, the monster will emerge from his hiding place and *devour* them. (*He leers*) When Tom arrives and summons him, I'll use you to distract his attention, so that *I* may sieze the sword, whilst Grendelgorm tears *him* to pieces. (*He laughs harshly*)

Princess (*bravely*) You'll never get away with it. Tom's more than a match for you *or* Grendelgorm.

Knave You think so, my proud Princess? (*He chuckles*) In a few moments we shall see who's right. Come. (*He holds out his hand*) We'll hide behind the tree.

Princess (*looking over his shoulder; delightedly*) Tom.

With a snarl of rage, the Knave turns to look

> *The Princess dashes off* DR

Knave (*turning back quickly and seeing her go*) Come back.

> *The Knave exits after her. After a moment, Jack, Kitty, the King, the Queen and the Chamberlain enter* DL

Jack (*looking around as he moves* C) Well this seems to be the end of the path, so we've probably arrived at the centre of the island.

Queen (*limping after him*) Thank goodness for that. I don't think I could manage another step.

King That's entirely your own fault, Matti. I said you'd end up suffering for your beliefs.

Chamberlain (*curious*) Which beliefs are those, Your Majesty?

Queen (*wrily*) I believed I could get my size six feet into these size four shoes.

Kitty (*sympathetically*) Never mind, Your Majesty. There's a fallen log at the foot of that tree, so why don't you have a little rest?

She helps the Queen to the log and seats her

Chamberlain I don't see any sign of Master Sprightly. Perhaps he's inside that cave? Should I go and ascertain, sire?

King Good idea, Chamberlain.

Jack Wait. If this *is* the centre of the island, that cave could well be the home of the guardian we were told about.

Chamberlain Oh. (*He eyes the cave nervously and edges away from it*)

Jack I think that just to be on the safe side, we'll have to take certain steps.

King Yes. Very long ones. Come on. (*He gets ready to leave*)

Queen (*chiding*) Now, now, Aloysius.

Kitty (*moving down to him*) It's no use our running away, Your Majesty. Not if we're going to defeat the Knave and get your kingdom back. We've got to stay here and give Tom all the help he needs.

Chamberlain (*resignedly*) I suppose she's right, sire. Your noble ancestors wouldn't have dreamed of leaving the battlefield at a moment like this.

King (*grimacing*) No. (*Bucking up*) They *did* like a good fight, though, didn't they? (*Proudly*) In the last two thousand years, they fought the Romans, the Vikings, the Normans, the Turks, the Spaniards, the Picts, Scots, Celts, Americans, French, Germans, Japanese *and* Italians.

Queen (*surprised*) Good gracious. Didn't they get on with *anybody*?

Jack (*suddenly*) Listen. Someone's coming.

They all turn to look

> *Tom enters cautiously* DL, *sword in hand and the cloak over his arm*

Kitty (*delightedly*) Tom. (*She hurries to him*)

Tom (*surprised*) Kitty. (*Seeing the others*) Everyone. How did *you* get here?

Jack We'll explain all that later. The important thing is that we're here to help you.

Tom (*wrily*) I'm afraid it's not me that's needing help at the moment. It's Marigold. She's been captured by the Knave and brought here to help him stop me finding Excalibur.

Everyone reacts

Queen (*upset*) Oh, whatever are we going to do?

Tom Don't worry, Your Majesty. The Fairy promised me no harm would come to the Princess. All *I* have to do is concentrate on getting the sword, and everything else can be left to her.

King Master Sprightly, save my daughter and get my kingdom back, and I'll make you the richest man in Nursery-rhyme Land, even if I have to sell the crown jewels to do it.

Tom Thank you, sire, but I don't want your money. Just your permission to marry the Princess – if she'll have me.

King Consider it given.

Tom (*delightedly*) In that case, I'll face a *thousand* guardians. (*Seriously*) Now quickly. I'd better get you all away from here. If Grendelgorm does come out of that cave, I want to be quite sure you'll all be safe.

Kitty Do you have a plan?

Tom Not really. But I do have this. (*He shows his cloak*)

Chamberlain Grendelgorm's a *bull*?

Tom No, no. Last night, Fairy Harmony placed a spell on it, and I've only to wear it to become instantly invisible. With any luck, I'll have the sword and be out of his reach before he even knows it's gone.

Jack Is there anything I can do to help?

Tom Just keep your eyes peeled for the Knave. Now follow me. I'll take you to a safe hiding place.

With much excitement, they follow Tom off DL *and exit*

Georgie (*off* R, *calling*) Aubergine? Auuuuuuuubergine?

He enters backwards

Where are you? (*To the audience*) Hiya, kids. Here, you haven't seen Aubergine, have you?

Audience reaction

Oh, ecky thump. I wonder where she's got to? (*Calling*) Aubergine? (*He sings*) When I'm calling you … oo … oo … oo … oo … oo … oo …

Dame (*off*) I will answer true … oo … oo … oo … oo … oo … oo.

Dame Sprightly enters from behind the tree, dressed in an "improvized" gown

Georgie (*gaping*) What on earth have you got on?

Dame (*beaming*) Do you like it? This is what I call my Atomic Bomb dress. It's got a fifty per cent fall out. (*She titters*) Here, you'll never guess what I've just found out.

Georgie What's that?

Dame Well, you see that tree over there? (*She indicates the Tree of Truth*) *That* is the famous Tree of Truth.

Georgie Honest? And what's it famous for?

Dame (*archly*) Legend has it, that if anyone sits down under that tree and tells a lie, an apple will fall down and hit them right on top of their head.

Georgie (*scornfully*) Gerraway. You don't expect me to believe that, do you?

Dame (*shrugging*) Please yourself.

Georgie You're pulling my leg, aren't you? (*To the audience*) Isn't she, kids? (*Audience reaction*) See.

Dame (*innocently*) I don't care what they say. I'm telling you, if you tell a lie, you'll get hit on the head by an apple.

Georgie All right, then. Come on. Prove it to me.

Dame Right.

They sit on the log, side by side

Now then. First question. Do you think that I'm conceited?

Georgie (*grinning at the audience*) Why should I think that?

Dame Well, girls as attractive and witty as I am usually are. (*She turns her head away from him and primps her hair*)

Georgie (*firmly*) No. I don't think you're conceited. (*He nods to audience*)

An apple falls and hits him on the head

Owwwwwwww. (*He rubs his head and looks up into the tree*)

Dame (*looking at him*) See. That jolly well serves you right. You told me a lie and got conked by a cooking apple. (*She turns smugly away*)

Georgie No I didn't. A mosquito bit me.

An apple falls and hits him on the head

Owwwwww. (*He rubs his head*)

Dame (*turning back to him, sharply*) That was another one, wasn't it?

Georgie Course it wasn't.

An apple falls and hits him on the head

Owwwwww. (*He jumps up rubbing his head*) Here, change places for a minute.

Dame Sprightly shrugs and moves over. Georgie sits on the other side of her

That's better. We've got a change of scenery now, haven't we?

Dame Mmmmmm. (*Sweetly*) Do you love me, Georgie? (*She turns her head away*)

Georgie opens his mouth to speak, then hesitates. He looks up into the tree for a moment, gives a quick glance at Dame Sprightly, then bites his lip and looks at the audience

I'm waiting.

He reaches behind the log and produces an old umbrella. Opening it up, he holds it over his head and grins at the audience

Georgie What a silly thing to ask me, Aubergine. Of course I love you.

He cowers under the umbrella. Dame Sprightly cocks her ear for the thud, but nothing happens

Dame (*uncertainly*) Did you say you *do* love me?

Georgie (*bolder*) Oh, yes. In fact I love you even more than I love (*names well-known sex symbol*).

Dame Sprightly reacts in surprise. Georgie cowers and waits for the apple, but again nothing happens

Dame (*delighted*) I can't believe it. (*She clutches her heart with glee*)

Georgie Would *I* lie to *you*? I think you're the most beautiful woman on earth.

Dame Sprightly is ecstatic. No apple falls

Dame (*to the audience*) Oh, girls. I've landed him. He's told the truth at last.

Chortling to himself with glee, Georgie moves the umbrella unintentionally. Three apples fall on his head in quick succession

Georgie Owwww. Owwww. Owwwwww. (*With a snort of disgust, he throws the brolly offstage*) I'm fed up of this. (*To Dame Sprightly*) Here, let *me* ask *you* a question. How old are you?

Dame (*after a slight hesitation*) Well, I'm as old as my tongue, and a little bit older than my teeth. (*She beams at him*)

Georgie Oh, no. Oh, no. I want to know how old you are in *years*.

Dame Oh. In years. (*She sighs*) Let me see, then. When Tommy Tucker was two years old, I was only one, and that made me half his age. Now he's sixty-four, I must still be half his age, so you can work it out for yourself.

Georgie (*amazed*) Thirty-two? You're *thirty-two*? (*He stands*)

Dame If you say so.

Georgie Never mind if *I* say so. I want *you* to say so. I want you to tell me you're thirty-two years old.

Dame (*after a long pause*) All right then. (*She looks up at the tree*) I'm (*she mouths the words silently*).

Georgie I can't hear you. Say it louder.

Dame (*whispering*) Thirty-two.

Georgie Louder.

Dame (*loudly*) I'm thirty-two.

Nothing happens

Georgie (*amazed*) I don't believe it. That must be the world's biggest lie and nothing's happened to you. How did you do it?

Dame Simple. (*She grins*) While you were wandering round looking for me, I glued all the other apples on to the tree with super-glue. (*She laughs*) I can tell as many lies as I like and not a single apple will fall on *me*. (*She rocks with laughter*)

There is a loud crack, and a huge branch falls off the tree and knocks her off the log. Georgie roars with laughter

Tom hurries on DL

Tom Mother. Georgie. Quick. You've got to get away from here. You're both in terrible danger.

Dame (*getting up*) Don't say the local drama critic's here tonight?

Tom No, no. I'm about to take the magic sword, and the moment I do so, the guardian will arrive. Now run.

Georgie Don't worry, Tom. I've just spotted the perfect hiding place. Come on, Aubergine.

Georgie grabs Dame Sprightly's hand and rushes her into the cave

Tom (*aghast*) Oh, no. You can't go in there. (*Calling*) Mother. Georgie. Come back.

Tom hurries into cave after them. Buckett and Spade enter DR

Buckett It's no use. We're absolutely lost.

Spade (*worried*) What are we going to do?

Buckett We'll have one final go at attracting somebody's attention. Fire into the air again. Just like you did a few minutes ago. Now we're out in the open, we stand a far better chance of being heard.

Spade (*weakly*) I can't. I threw the bow away when I found out I'd got no more arrows.

Buckett (*disgustedly*) Well that's it, then, isn't it? We're going to be stuck on this island for the rest of our lives, just like Robinson Crusoe.

Spade *Who?*

Buckett Robinson Crusoe. (*Exasperated*) Oh, come on. Even *you* must have heard of Crusoe.

Spade (*light dawning*) Oh, yes. Wasn't he that famous opera singer?

Buckett (*wincing*) I give up. (*Patiently*) Doesn't it bother you to know that you'll probably never set eyes on a pretty girl again?

Spade Why should it? I don't have anything to do with girls, anyway.

Buckett (*puzzled*) Why not?

Spade Because they're bad for your health, aren't they?

Buckett (*amazed*) How can girls be bad for your health? Girls are sugar and spice and all things nice.

Spade I know. And that means they must be fattening. And everybody knows being fat isn't healthy.

Buckett snatches off his hat and beats Spade over the head with it

Princess Marigold hurries on DR

Princess (*breathlessly*) Oh, please. You've got to help me . . .

The Knave enters behind her

(*Recognizing Buckett and Spade*) Oh . . . (*She turns to run*)

Knave (*triumphantly*) Ahaaaaa. (*He leaps forward and grabs her arm*)

Princess (*struggling*) Let go of me. Let go.

Buckett (*relieved*) Boss. Cor, are we glad to see your ugly mu—— I mean to see you.

Spade Yeah. We should have known *you'd* turn up to save us. (*He beams*)

Knave Save you? (*Scornfully*) You bungling fools. I wouldn't lift a finger to save *your* miserable hides.

Buckett ⎱
Spade ⎰ (*together; startled*) *Eh?*

Knave As soon as the magic sword is mine, I'll have no further use for idiots like you.

Buckett (*huffily*) Well if that's all the thanks we're going to get, you can keep your rotten old job.

Spade (*indignantly*) Yes. As soon as you've taken us back to England, you can give us the money we're owed, and we'll say "Cheerio".

Knave Taken you back to England? (*He laughs harshly*) You can stay here and rot, for all I care. Now stand aside. I have business to attend to.

Dragging the Princess behind him, he pushes past them and exits L

Spade (*upset*) I knew this was going to happen. I knew it. Nothing's gone right for us since we upset that Fairy in Act One.

Buckett You're right. She warned us what a nasty old villain he was. Oh, if only we'd listened to her.

Fairy Harmony enters R

Fairy   How very true – and now you reap reward for your great crime.
Upon this isle you're doomed to stay, at least for quite some time.
Though *if* Tom gets the magic sword, and *truly* you repent,
Give promise to be good henceforth, I might – perhaps – relent.

Spade Oh, yes, Missis Fairy. We'll do anything you ask. Anything at all.

Buckett Just get us off this island, and we'll never be wicked again.

Fairy   Your future rests in the hands of chance. The fateful hour is here.
Come, Tom. Your destiny awaits. Excalibur doth now appear.

She waves her wand. There is a flash and the magic sword appears in the centre of the Tree of Truth. Buckett and Spade back DL *quickly*

Fairy Harmony exits R. *There is a simultaneous bellow of rage from inside the cave. A moment later, Dame Sprightly, Georgie and Tom come running out*

Tom (*urgently*) Hide. Quickly.

There is another roar of rage. Dame and Georgie hide behind the Tree of Truth. Tom hurriedly puts on his cloak, and waits, sword in hand

Buckett (*startled*) Where's he gone? (*He looks around baffled*)

Spade He's vanished.

With a great roar, Grendelgorm appears in the cave entrance

The Lights dim. Buckett and Spade are petrified with fear and try to climb the proscenium arch. The monster looks around and sees them. With a growl he sets off towards them. Tom quickly jumps forward and stabs him with his sword. With a cry of pain, Grendelgorm turns round. Buckett and Spade dash over to

DR. *Tom scuttles behind the monster again and gives him another jab. Again, the monster howls and turns. This is repeated*

Suddenly the Knave appears DL, *dragging the Princess*

Knave (*to her*) See how Grendelgorm destroys your dashing hero ... (*He suddenly realizes*) Ten thousand curses. The boy is invisible. This is all the doing of that interfering Fairy, but I'll soon put a stop to it. (*He casts a spell in the direction of the fighters*)
Princess (*suddenly seeing him*) Tom ...
Tom (*startled*) Marigold. (*He turns to look at her*)

Grendelgorm lashes out at him and his sword is knocked from his hand

(*Dismayed*) Oh, no.

He steps back as the monster moves towards him

Knave (*triumphantly*) Grendelgorm wins.
Tom Not yet, he doesn't.

He dodges out of Grendelgorm's path, but is unable to reach his sword. As Grendelgorm pursues him, the Knave pushes Marigold aside and begins heading cautiously for the magic sword

Princess (*realizing*) He's after the sword. Stop him.

Sneering, the Knave reaches out for it. As he does so, Buckett and Spade launch themselves at him

Knave (*struggling furiously*) Let go, you fools. Let go.

Seeing his chance, Tom avoids Grendelgorm and grabs the magic sword. With the aid of it, he drives the monster back and finally stabs it

With a loud cry of pain, Grendelgorm staggers into the cave. His death cry is heard

The Lights come up to full again

Tom Grendelgorm is dead, and the sword is mine. (*He holds it aloft*)

The Princess hurries to Tom and they embrace

Everyone, except Fairy Harmony, rushes on joyously

(*To the Knave*) And now to deal with you. (*He points the sword at him*)
Knave (*terrified*) Mercy. Mercy. (*He falls to his knees*)

Fairy Harmony enters, smiling

Fairy   Brave Tom, your quest is now fulfilled. The Knave admits defeat.
His magic power your sword destroys, which makes his downfall
     quite complete.
Our Fairy Queen renews her spell to keep you all content,
And free from knavish curs like *this* (*she indicates the Knave*)
Who now returns to banishment.
All smile with satisfaction

Just one more thing remains to say ere home you go tonight.
The treasure of great Grendelgorm is yours by victor's right.
Tom (*delightedly*) You mean, I'm rich?

Everyone looks delighted

Fairy   Beyond your very wildest dreams, so in your pockets dig.
A penny piece I'll ask of you (*she holds out her hand*)
For purchase of that "stolen" pig.

All laugh. Tom fumbles in his pocket for a coin

Now back to England and Nursery-rhyme,
Where we'll meet again when the wedding bells chime.

All cheer loudly. The Lights fade quickly and the lane cloth comes across

SCENE 6

Back in Nursery-rhyme Land

The Lights come up to full on the song sheet, or as required

SCENE 7

The Palace of Hearts

The Lights come up to full on the palace interior. There is an optional dance for the Choristers. Following this they exit

As the finale music starts the cast walk down as follows:

Babes
Choristers
Herald and Grendelgorm (*carrying the monster head*)
Captain and Pieman
Chamberlain
Fairy Harmony and Knave of Hearts
Jack and Kitty
Buckett and Spade
King and Queen
Dame Sprightly and Georgie
Tom and Princess Marigold

When all are assembled, the finale music ends and Tom steps forward

Tom   The tale is told. It's time to part.
We hope you liked our fun.
So now farewell from cast and crew
Of Tom, the Piper's son.

There is a reprise of any popular song from the show at the end of which———

— the CURTAIN falls

FURNITURE AND PROPERTY LIST

PROLOGUE

On stage: Brazier

Personal: **Fairy Harmony:** wand (used throughout)

ACT 1
Scene 1

On stage: Cottage cut-out with practical door

Off stage: Large bundle of sticks **(Tom)**
Small bundles of firewood **(Tom)**

Personal: **Tom:** pipes hanging from waist (used throughout)
Georgie: paper bag containing large pair of bloomers with hole
Dame Sprightly: coin

Scene 2

On stage: Nil

Off stage: Open letter, shopping bag containing pheasant or chicken **(Dame Sprightly)**
Open letter **(Dame Sprightly)**
Shopping bag containing pheasant or chicken **(Georgie)**

Personal: **Georgie:** £5 note

Scene 3

On stage: Nil

Personal: **Fayreground Vendors:** display trays of toys, balloons, doughnuts, candy floss etc.
Pieman: large display tray piled high with pastry pigs
Jack: money

Scene 4

On stage: £1 note on floor

Off stage: Few bundles of sticks **(Dame Sprightly)**
Half a pastry pig **(Tom)**

SCENE 5

On stage: 2 thrones on dais

Off stage: Pieman's costume in bundle **(Kitty)**
Schoolboy's costume in bundle **(Georgie)**
Cloak **(Page-boy)**
Sword on velvet cushion **(Page-boy)**

Personal: **Queen Mattiwilda:** small pasteboard card

ACT II
SCENE 1

On stage: Inn cut-out with practical door

Personal: **Captain:** cutlass (used throughout), bag of gold
Georgie: large diamond ring in pocket
Knave: royal crown
Queen: photograph

SCENE 2

On stage: Nil

Personal: **Dame Sprightly:** letter

SCENE 3

On stage: Giant palm trees
Log

Off stage: Baskets **(King, Queen, Chamberlain)**
Pails **(Jack, Kitty)**

Personal: **Princess Marigold:** handkerchief
Tom: cloak, sword

SCENE 4

On stage: Nil

Personal: **Tom:** cloak, sword

SCENE 5

On stage: Cave entrance
Overhanging tree with "apples" and detachable branch. *In tree:* magic
sword (see Author's Note on page vii). *At base:* fallen log with umbrella
behind it
Rocks
Trees
Bushes
Large trays of assorted foods (for **Serving-wenches**)

Personal: **Chefs:** wooden spoons or ladles
          Tom: cloak and sword (used throughout), coin in pocket
          Buckett: hat

SCENE 6

On stage: Song sheet or as required

SCENE 7

Off stage: Full set or as required

LIGHTING PLOT

Practical fittings required: glowing brazier
Several simple interior and exterior settings

PROLOGUE

To open: Eerie multi-coloured effect on lane cloth with dim glow from brazier

Cue 1	**Knave:** "Speak, I beseech thee."	(Page 1)
	Brazier glows brighter	
Cue 2	**Knave:** " I shall have the answer."	(Page 1)
	Brazier flares up very brightly	
Cue 3	**Fairy Harmony** enters R	(Page 1)
	White spot on Fairy Harmony	
Cue 4	**Fairy:** "Because it's *out*."	(Page 2)
	Snap off brazier glow	
Cue 5	**Fairy Harmony** exits	(Page 2)
	Fade white spot	
Cue 6	**Knave** laughs triumphantly	(Page 2)
	Black-out	

ACT 1

To open: Bright sunny morning effect

Cue 7	**Georgie** dashes off, chased by **Dame**	(Page 8)
	Dim lighting	
Cue 8	**Knave:** ". . . two black-hearted villains deliver to me."	(Page 8)
	Lighting flickers, then Black-out	
Cue 9	As **Buckett** and **Spade** tumble on to the stage	(Page 8)
	Bring up bright sunny morning effect	
Cue 10	After Song 3, **Tom** and the **Princess** exit	(Page 12)
	Fade to Black-out, then bring up full general lighting on lane cloth	
Cue 11	All shriek with rage and chase **Georgie** off	(Page 16)
	Black-out	
Cue 12	To open Scene 3	(Page 16)
	Bring up full general lighting	
Cue 13	As everyone exits after Song 5	(Page 19)
	Dim lighting	

Cue 14	As **Knave** exits *Bring up full general lighting*	(Page 19)
Cue 15	**Buckett** and **Spade** are left behind, chortling *Quick fade to Black-out*	(Page 25)
Cue 16	To open SCENE 4 *Bring up full general lighting on lane cloth*	(Page 25)
Cue 17	The **Villagers** drag **Tom** off and everyone exits *Quick fade to Black-out*	(Page 27)
Cue 18	To open SCENE 5 *Bring up full interior lighting*	(Page 27)
Cue 19	Crash of thunder *Lighting flickers*	(Page 32)
Cue 20	**Fairy:** "Begone." (*She waves her wand*) *White spot on knave*	(Page 32)
Cue 21	**Knave, Buckett** and **Spade** exit *Fade white spot*	(Page 33)

ACT II

To open: General daylight effect

Cue 22	**Dame Sprightly** drags **Georgie** off UR *Dim lighting*	(Page 39)
Cue 23	The **Knave** exits behind inn *Bring up lighting to full*	(Page 39)
Cue 24	The **Princess** collides with the **Knave** *Dim lighting*	(Page 40)
Cue 25	The **Knave** and the **Princess** exit *Bring up lighting to full*	(Page 41)
Cue 26	The **Sailors** swoop on the party and everyone exits *Quick fade to Black-out*	(Page 42)
Cue 27	To open SCENE 2 *Bring up full daylight effect*	(Page 42)
Cue 28	**Georgie:** "It's broad daylight." *Dim lighting quickly and bring up full moon effect*	(Page 45)
Cue 29	**Dame** and **Georgie** dash off pursued by **Captain** *Black-out*	(Page 46)
Cue 30	To open SCENE 3 *Bring up dappled sunlight effect, then dusk gradually falling*	(Page 46)
Cue 31	**Gorilla** exits after **Georgie** *Black-out*	(Page 52)
Cue 32	To open SCENE 4 *Bring up evening effect on lane cloth*	(Page 52)

EFFECTS PLOT

ACT I

Cue 1   **Knave:** "... two black-hearted villains deliver to me."   (Page 8)
Flash

Cue 2   At the end of Song 4   (Page 16)
Fanfare

Cue 3   The **Knave** raises his arm and casts a spell   (Page 32)
Crash of thunder, followed by sound of rushing wind

ACT II

Cue 4   At the end of Song 13   (Page 46)
Flash

Cue 5   **Dame:** "... will fall on *me*." (*She rocks with laughter*)   (Page 57)
Loud crack

Cue 6   **Fairy Harmony** waves her wand   (Page 59)
Flash